NCERT
QUESTIONS-ANSWERS

English Core

Textbooks : Flamingo (Prose & Poetry)
& Vistas (Supplementary Reader)

CLASS
12

NCERT

QUESTIONS-ANSWERS

English Core

Textbooks : Flamingo (Prose & Poetry)
& Vistas (Supplementary Reader)

by

Megha Karnani

Arihant Prakashan (School Division Series)

卐 Administrative & Production Offices

Regd. Office

'Ramchhaya' 4577/15, Agarwal Road, Darya Ganj, New Delhi -110002
Tele: 011- 47630600, 43518550

卐 Head Office

Kalindi, TP Nagar, Meerut (UP) - 250002
Tel: 0121-7156203, 7156204

卐 Sales & Support Offices

Agra, Ahmedabad, Bengaluru, Bareilly, Chennai, Delhi, Guwahati, Hyderabad, Jaipur, Jhansi, Kolkata, Lucknow, Nagpur & Pune.

卐 ISBN 978-93-27198-21-8

PO No : TXT-XX-XXXXXXX-X-XX

Published by Arihant Publications (India) Ltd.

For further information about the books published by Arihant, log on to www.arihantbooks.com or e-mail at info@arihantbooks.com

Follow us on   

Preface

Feeling the immense importance and value of NCERT books, we are presenting this book, having the NCERT Exercises Solutions.

A student can think to attain good marks in the literature only when he is well versed with the NCERT books; **'Flamingo' & 'Vistas'** and has prepared all the chapters alongwith their questions in a good manner. The questions asked in this section are usually from NCERT books, so by preparing all the questions of the text books students can expect very good marks in this section. This book is designed in such a way that it will show the way to the students how to write the answers of the Textbook-based Questions. All the questions given in all the chapters of 'Flamingo' & 'Vistas' have been covered in detail.

We have introduced some **Additional Features** alongwith the Questions-Answers which are given below:

The Story Retold At the start of each prose chapter, **detailed summary with outlines** have been given. By studying it, students can understand the chapter and can make them well–versed with it and will be able to answer all possible questions concerned to a particular chapter whether it is **Long Answer Type** or **Short Answer Type**.

Stanzawise Explanation At the start of each poem, **detailed explanation of each and every stanza** of the poem have been given. By studying it, students can understand the chapter and can make them well–versed with it and will be able to answer all possible questions concerned to a particular chapter whether it is **Extract Based Questions** or **Short Answer Type Questions**.

Intext Questions The intext questions given in between the chapters have also been thoroughly dealt with to enhance the **critical ability** and **understanding** of the students.

With the hope that this book will be of great help to the students, we wish great success to our readers.

Megha Karnani

Contents

Flamingo-Prose

Flamingo-Poetry

Vistas-Supplementary

The Last Lesson

Alphonse Daudet

Introduction

The Last Lesson by Alphonse Daudet was written in the days of the Franco-Prussian War in which France was defeated by Prussia led by Bismark. The French district of Alsace and Lorraine passed into Prussian hands. It showcases the fact that the oppressor wants not only territory but also dominates over the language and culture of a particular country thus, taking away even the identity of the subjugated people.

The Story Retold

Franz had not prepared his lesson; sees a crowd in front of bulletin-board

The author was late for school and dreaded scolding from his teacher, Mr M Hamel who was to question them that day on participles. The narrator had not learnt his lessons. It was a bright day and he felt tempted to stay back from school and enjoy the day but somehow he resisted the temptation to do so. While he was passing by the town hall, he saw a crowd in front of the bulletin-board. Since the war was on, all the bad news had come from that board. As he was hurrying past, the blacksmith called out to him and said there was plenty of time to reach the school in time.

To his surprise; his teacher is kind to him

When the author reached school, he was very surprised at the eerie silence that surrounded the school. It seemed more like a

Sunday than a working day. He had depended on the commotion to enter the class unnoticed but to his surprise everyone was already in their places and he had to go before everybody. What surprised him even more was that instead of scolding him the teacher was kind and told him to take his place.

M Hamel is in his special attire; the atmosphere of the class is not the same

After settling, the narrator, Franz noticed that the teacher was wearing his beautiful green coat, his frilled shirt and his little black silk cap with embroidery on it. This attire was worn by M Hamel only on inspection or prize days. The atmosphere that day was very solemn and what surprised him most was when he saw the village elders sitting in the class on the last benches. Everyone was sad. One of the persons sitting there was old Hauser who had even brought an old primer which he thumbed at the edges. He held it open on his knees.

Taken aback; regrets when teacher says it is the last lesson

The narrator wondered at the changes when suddenly M Hamel mounted his chair and announced that it was their last French lesson as the order had come from Berlin that only German will be taught in the schools of Alsace and Lorriane. The narrator was shocked to hear this and suddenly those books which had seemed a burden became very dear to him. He regretted not having learnt his lessons. Now the narrator understood why Mr Hamel had put on his Sunday clothes and why the villagers were attending the class that day. It was their way of thanking the master for his commendable service of forty years and showing respect to their country.

They also regretted missing the school so often. When the class started, the narrator heard his name being called out to recite the rules of the participles which he was unable to do as he got stuck on the first word. He felt very disgusted with himself at his failure to do so. Mr Hamel said he wouldn't scold him for he was, as it is, feeling so bad about it. Everyday learning had been postponed to the next day and now there was no time left to learn. He further said that they would be mocked by people for calling themselves French although they couldn't speak or write their own language.

Fumbles while reciting participles; is ashamed

Further, Mr Hamel says even many parents had preferred to send their children to work than to school. Then he confesses that he too was to blame because many times he had given a holiday when he wanted to go fishing. Mr Hamel said that French was the most beautiful language in the world. It was the most clearest and logical. He then opened the book and explained a grammar lesson to them. The writer was surprised at himself for he understood the lesson very well. Also Mr Hamel had explained the lesson more patiently than ever. It almost seemed as if in one go he wanted to give them all that he knew. The grammar lesson was followed by a writing lesson. That day Mr Hamel had new copies for them in which it was written in beautiful round hand — France, Alsace, France, Alsace. They looked like little flags floating everywhere in the classroom. All the children worked seriously and quietly. Suddenly, the writer heard the pigeons cooing and wondered will they be also made to sing in German.

Mr Hamel makes people realise the importance of mother tongue

While the class was doing their writing assignment, M Hamel sat motionless in his chair staring at all the things as if he wanted to remember just how everything looked in that little school room.

Since M Hamel had started the school forty years ago, nothing had changed except the desk and chairs had worn off and the trees had grown taller. The narrator wonders that it must be heart-breaking for him to hear his sister moving the trunks in the room above, packing to leave the country next day.

Mr Hamel is an epitome of patience that day; a patriot to the core

Mr M Hamel was very patient that day. When it was the chance of the babies to chant the alphabet, even the old villagers joined in. Their voice trembled with emotion. At twelve all of them could hear the Prussians returning from drill. At this overcome with emotion, M Hamel went to the blackboard and wrote, *Vive La France* (Long Live France). He then leaned against the wall and dismissed the class with a gesture.

To sum up, we can say that the story is a wake-up call for all those people who keep on postponing things endlessly. Something like this happened with the natives of Alsace. They had to forego learning their mother tongue. In the same vein, the story extrapolates the fact that war makes man inhuman and insensitive to the feelings of others.

Exercises

Think as you read (Page 7)

Question 1. What was Franz expected to be prepared with for school that day?
Delhi 2011

Answer Franz was expected to be prepared with his lesson on participles. M Hamel, his French teacher, had announced that he would question the class on participles. But Franz didn't know even the first word about them.

Question 2. What did Franz notice that was unusual about the school that day?
Delhi 2012

Answer Franz noticed many unusual things about school that day. First, normally when the school began there was much commotion, which was missing that day. Second, his teacher, M Hamel, had worn his ceremonial clothes. Third, which was most unusual, the village people were sitting quietly on the back benches, which were usually empty on other days.

Question 3. What had been put up on the bulletin-board?
Delhi 2011

Answer An order that had come from Berlin had been put up on the bulletin-board. The order was that from the next day onwards, only German would be taught in the schools of Alsace and Lorraine. The new teacher for German would join the school from the following day.

Think as you read (Page 8)

Question 1. What changes did the order from Berlin cause on school that day?

Answer The order from Berlin caused the French language to be stopped from being taught in the schools of Alsace and Lorraine from that day. It stated that only German will be taught in the schools there from then onwards.

This meant that M Hamel, the French teacher, would have to leave. This also caused the elder villagers to attend the school for the last lesson in French.

Question 2. How did Franz's feelings about M Hamel and school change?

Answer Franz's feelings about M Hamel and school changed when M Hamel told the students about the order from Berlin and that it was their last French lesson. Franz forgot about his teacher's ruler and crankiness; instead, he started liking M Hamel, as he was being separated from M Hamel forever. His feelings towards his school also changed, as he did not want to give up his books and lessons, as they seemed to be old friends.

Understanding the text   (Page 9)

Question 1. The people in this story suddenly realise how precious their language is to them. What shows you this? Why does this happen?

Answer When the order came from Berlin that henceforth only German will be taught in schools, people realised that it was the last day to learn their mother tongue. To show their affection for the language, many elderly people came to attend school, occupying the last benches which usually remained vacant. Franz regretted having not learnt the participles when M Hamel suddenly appraised them of the fact that they will become a laughing stock. It is their identity, the 'key' to their prison. The strongest evidence of how important is language comes from M Hamel's mesmerizing last lesson. This happened because of the French language being banned in Alsace and Lorraine.

Question 2. Franz thinks, "Will they make them sing in German, even the pigeons?" What could this mean?

Answer In the Franco–Prussian war of 1870, when France was defeated and the districts of Alsace and Lorraine passed into the hands of the Prussians, orders came from Berlin that only German will be taught in schools. A new master would be coming to teach German. So it was the last lesson in French. Franz and all others present there felt sad and regretted putting off things at a later date. Just then the pigeons on the roof started cooing which made him think will the same orders come for animal kingdom too? Will they also have to forget their own language and learn German?

This points out to the mindset of man in general and conquerors specifically. Man has an intense desire to subjugate others. No wonder, he wants to enslave animals also. Just dominating and ruling over territory is not enough. Captors want to rule over minds as well. That's the reason why they impose their language on the oppressed. Linguistic chauvinism is the beginning of servitude.

In a nutshell, we can say that Franz's question is typical because it showcases the streak of authority and supremacy inherent in man. Given a chance, man might not even think twice before invading the sacred realm of Gods!

Talking about the text   (Page 9)

Question 1. "When a people are enslaved, as long as they hold fast to their language, it is as if they had the key to their prison." Explain.

Answer Subjugation of a country deprives people of their identity and freedom. One is subjected to restrictions in his/her own land. The worst part is when one has to abide by the diktats of the oppressor.

In these testing times it is only our mother tongue that binds us together. It becomes a weapon against the tyrants who have forcibly moved into a country. The teacher, M Hamel, is perfectly right when he says that it is a 'key to their prison'. Language is a catalyst that initiates and sustains the freedom movement. So he reminds his countrymen of the importance of language; it is their identity and only when they fight for it will the future generations remember that they have been enslaved. It is only then they will carry the torch of freedom further.

India, Bangladesh, South Africa are some of the examples in history where the conquered people had their language taken away from them and another language imposed on themselves.

Question 2. What happens to a linguistic minority in a state? How do you think they can keep their language alive? For example: Punjabis in Bangalore, Tamilians in Mumbai, Kannadigas in Delhi or Gujaratis in Kolkata.

Answer A linguistic minority in a state cannot exercise linguistic skills like the natives of the state. At the workplace and educational organisations, English / Hindi or any other link language helps a lot to cope with the work and learning process. But, when it comes to understanding the basic norms of society, in order to socialise, they face linguistic barriers during communication.

To keep their language alive, the linguistic minorities can form small communities where they can celebrate their festivals as per their traditions. They can also continue to speak their native language in their homes and make their children learn the language. They should also try to visit their native places at regular intervals to stay close to their roots.

Question 3. Is it possible to carry pride in one's language too far? Do you know what 'linguistic chauvinism' means?

Answer Yes, it is possible to carry pride in one's language too far if one is fond of one's own language at the cost of others. Indifference towards other languages is not healthy in a democracy like India. When the sense of belonging to one's own language crosses the line between 'pride' and 'being proud', it becomes linguistic chauvinism. If people feel good about their languages and traditions, they must have tolerance for other languages too.

Everybody has the right to follow the religion as well as speak the language as per their desire. In fact, it is denigrating to distort the names of communities, like Bongs for Bengalis, Gujjus for Gujratis and so on.

Working with words   (Page 9-10)

Question 1. English is a language that contains words from many other languages. This inclusiveness is one of the reasons it is now a world language. For example

Petite	—	French
Kindergarten	—	German
Capital	—	Latin
Democracy	—	Greek
Bazaar	—	Hindi

Find out the origin of the following words

(i) Tycoon   (ii) tulip   (iii) logo   (iv) bandicoot

(v) barbecue   (vi) veranda   (vii) robot   (viii) Zero

(ix) ski   (x) trek

Answer

Word	Origin
(i) Tycoon	Japanese (taikun)
(ii) Tulip	French (tulipe)
(iii) Logo	German (logos)
(iv) Bandicoot	Telugu (pandikokku)
(v) Barbecue	Spanish (barbacoa)
(vi) Veranda	Portugese (veranda)
(vii) Robot	Czech (robota)
(viii) Zero	Arabic (cipher)
(ix) Ski	Norwegian
(x) Trek	Dutch (trekken)

Question 2. Notice the underlined words in these sentences and tick the option that best explains their meaning

(a) "What a thunderclap these words were to me!"

The words were
(i) loud and clear
(ii) startling and unexpected
(iii) pleasant and welcome

(b) "When people are enslaved, as long as they hold fast to their language it is as if they had the key to their prison".

It is as if they have the key to the prison as long as they

    (i) do not lose their language.
    (ii) are attached to their language.
    (iii) quickly learn the conqueror's language.

(c) Don't go so fast, you will get to your school in plenty of time.

    You will get to your school
    (i) very late
    (ii) too early
    (iii) early enough

(d) I never saw him look so tall

    M Hamel
    (i) had grown physically taller
    (ii) seemed very confident
    (iii) stood on the chair

Answer   (a) (i) loud and clear
          (b) (ii) are attached to their language
          (c) (iii) early enouth
          (d) (iii) stood on the chair

2

Lost Spring
(Stories of Stolen Childhood)
Anees Jung

Introduction

Anees Jung was born in 1964 at Rourkela. She spent her childhood and adolescence in Hyderabad. She has authored several books and has been an editor and columnist for major newspapers in India and abroad. The following is an excerpt that has been taken from her book tilted, 'Lost Spring : Stories of Stolen Childhood'.

The Story Retold

"Sometimes I Find a Rupee in The Garbage"

Author meets Saheb; the ragpicker

Saheb is seen by the author everyday searching for 'gold' in the garbage in the neighbouring vicinity. His family hails from the green fields in Bangladesh which they left a long time ago as they had been swept away due to storms.

The author on meeting Saheb wants to know why he doesn't go to school. To this he replies that there is no school in his neighbourhood and if a school is built then he would definitely go there. The author jokingly promises to open a school. This promise was like the many promises which are made to poor children like him, never to be fulfilled. The author is embarrassed when Saheb walks up to her one day to know if the school had been built.

Irony in Saheb's name; the enigma of remaining barefoot

One day, the author asks him his name. She sees irony in the fact that his name is 'Saheb-e-Alam' which means Lord of the universe but he is unaware of it and roams about in the streets with his friends. Most of them do not wear chappals. When the author inquires about the reason one says his mother did not bring them down from the shelf. Another says he only wants to wear shoes. While travelling across the country, the author has noticed many people moving barefoot. One explanation is that it is a tradition in a country steeped in poverty. The author wonders if it is only an excuse to hide their never ending poverty.

Author ponders on question; why are ragpickers still shoeless?

Anees Jung gets back in time and ponders upon how far we have progressed. She is reminded of a man who as a young boy would go to the temple and pray for a pair of shoes. Thirty years later when the author visited his town and the temple, behind the temple was the residence of the new priest. Some red and white chairs were kept in its courtyard and a boy was sitting there. He was wearing socks and shoes. The writer was reminded of the boy who prayed that he should never lose his shoes. But she is pained by the fact that the ragpickers were still shoeless.

Ragpickers' bastion—Seemapuri ; how garbage is 'gold'?

The writer speaks of Seemapuri which, though at the periphery of Delhi, is miles away from it. The place is occupied by squatters from Bangladesh back in 1971. They live in mud structures with roofs of tin and tarpaulin. The place has no drainage system or running water. More than 10000 ragpickers have been living here for the past thirty years. They have no identity, yet they have valid ration cards and their names are on the voters' list. Not having any identity does not bother them as long as they have food and don't have to sleep on empty stomachs. They have forgotten the green fields of their country as they were unable to subsist on them. They pitch their tents wherever they find food. To survive in Seemapuri, they have to pick rags which is 'gold' to them as it is their means of livelihood. Garbage to children has a different connotation. Saheb says sometimes he finds a ten rupee note or a coin in it. So, for children garbage is wrapped in wonder.

An instance of a child's longing for a normal childhood

The author next sees an instance of a child's longing for a normal childhood. One morning, she sees Saheb ouside the neighbourhood club watching tennis. He was wearing tennis shoes which were probably discarded by a rich boy. These shoes mismatched with faded clothes. Though the shoes had a hole, it did not bother Saheb. For him it was a dream come true.

How Saheb loses his freedom?

One morning, the author met Saheb when he was walking to the milk booth. He was carrying a steel canister. He told the author that he was now working at a tea stall and was paid rupees eight hundred plus his meals. He did not look happy. Infact his face had lost its earlier carefree look. The steel canister seemed heavier than the plastic bag he carried earlier. Saheb felt its burden for he had lost his freedom. The canister belonged to the owner of the tea stall where he worked now, whereas the sack was his own. At that time at least he was his own master.

"I Want to Drive a Car"

Mukesh; a child labourer in a bangle-making unit, Firozabad

In Firozabad, the author comes across Mukesh, a child labourer in a glass factory who wishes to be a motor mechanic. The author wants to know if he has any knowledge about cars. He says he will learn to drive a car. Mukesh belongs to a family which is engaged in bangle making like many other families. Firozabad is the hub of India's glass blowing industry where generation after generation has been involved in this business.

Author encounters bad living conditions; grinding poverty in Mukesh's house

The author comments on the ignorance of the people of Firozabad who involve their children in this industry at a very early age, least realising that it is illegal for children to work. If the law is enforced, almost 20000 children would be out of those hot furnaces. Mukesh is very happy when the author wishes to go to his house. He proudly tells the author that his house is being rebuilt. They walk through stinking lanes which are choked with garbage. They go past homes with crumbled walls, houses with no windows where families of humans and animals co-exist. They finally enter a half-built shack, one part of which is thatched with dead grass. Food was being cooked on a firewood stove by a frail, young woman. She was Mukesh's elder brother's wife. She is the *bahu* of the house. When Mukesh's father enters, she gently brings the veil closer to her face as it is the custom that daughters-in-law should cover their face before male elders. Mukesh's father has worked hard all his life, first as a tailor and then as a bangle maker. Still he has been unable to renovate his house or send his two sons to schools. The irony is, in spite of all this he has just managed to teach them the art of bangle making.

Mukesh's grandmother's view; it is destiny that can't be altered

Mukesh's grandmother believes in destiny. She has seen her husband going blind, polishing the glass bangles. Every yard and every street of Firozabad is full of bangles of all colours. The bangles, when ready, are piled on four wheeled hand carts which are pushed through the narrow streets by young men to be sent to the towns. She firmly believes that the art of bangle making is a God given lineage that cannot be escaped from. Young boys and girls of the city are seen sitting with their fathers and mothers near flickering lamps welding pieces of coloured glass. Their eyes are more adjusted to the dark in which they work. That is why they end up losing their eyesight early in life.

Savita; the tragic irony of being a girl child labourer & then a bride

Savita is a young girl dressed in pink. She sits with her parents soldering the pieces of glass. Even in the dark, her hands move very fast. At her age, she does not realise the importance of the bangles in the life of an Indian woman. This realisation will dawn upon her the day she gets married. There, a tinge of irony here because eventually all girl child labourers will become brides and wear the bangles. The old lady who is sitting next to her has lost her eyesight but has bangles on her wrist as her husband is alive. She complains of their poverty. In spite of the hard work put in they had not had enough to eat. Her husband complains of only being able to make a house for themselves.

The vicious circle of poverty; nexus between the police, politicians and money lenders

A common complaint of every family involved in the bangle making business is that there is no money to eat. The young repeat the complaint of their elders. Nothing has changed in the city over a period of time, all initiatives and dreams of the youth have got lost in hardwork.

The author suggests to a group to form co-operatives to save themselves from the vicious circle of the middlemen. The author is informed by the people there that if they get organised, they would be beaten by the police and put in jails. These people have no leader nor the awareness. They are caught in the ruthless cycle of poverty, aversion, greed and injustice.

The author feels they are caught in two distinct worlds. One is the family caught in the clutches of poverty and secondly, the stigma of caste. These people are caught in the vicious circle of sahukars, middlemen, policemen, bureaucrats and politicians. It is because of these people that the child is weighed down with responsibilities at such a tender age. He in turn accepts it as naturally as his father did. None dares to deviate.

The author sees that daring spirit and never-say-die attitude in Mukesh and hopes he will fulfil his dream. Mukesh insists on being a motor mechanic. He is willing to walk a long way to the garage to give wings to his dreams. At the same time, Mukesh is firmly rooted in the earth. He does not dream of flying aeroplanes. Anees Jung feels, may be this is due to the fact that few planes fly over Firozabad.

Exercises

Think as you read (Page 16)

Question 1. What is Saheb looking for in the garbage dumps? Where is he and where has he come from?

Answer Saheb is looking for 'gold' in the garbage dumps. Gold here means anything valuable like metal scraps, used things or stray coins and currency notes. Presently he lives in Seemapuri which is on the outskirts of Delhi. He and his family have come from the green fields of Dhaka which they left long ago.

Question 2. What explanations does the author offer for the children not wearing footwear?

Answer The children are always seen bare footed due to perpetual poverty of their families. Various explanations are offered to hide their condition. One says he only wants to wear shoes, the other child says his mother did not bring them down from the shelf. Some don't wear due to tradition. The author feels all these are just excuses to hide their perpetual poverty.

Question 3. Is Saheb happy working at the tea stall? Explain.

Answer No, Saheb is not happy working at the tea stall. He is being paid ₹ 800 but his face has lost the carefree look. Now, he is no more his own master. The steel canister seems much heavier than the plastic bag which he carried over his shoulders. He is no less than a bonded labourer accountable for each and every action if his.

Think as you read   (Page 19)

Question 1. What makes the city of Firozabad famous?

Answer Firozabad is famous for its bangles industry. It is the hub of India's glass blowing industry. Here, families have spent generations working around the furnaces, welding glass, making bangles for all the women as a symbol of auspiciousness and marriage.

Question 2. Mention the hazards of working in the glass bangles industry.

Answer The glass bangles industry offers very unhealthy environment to the people working in them. They have to work in the glass furnaces with high temperature in dingy cells without the basic amenities. Workers including child labourers, lose sight at an early age due to bad posture and incredibly long working hours.

Question 3. How is Mukesh's attitude to his situation different from that of his family?

Answer Mukesh's grandmother, father, elder brother, all believe that it is their 'god-given lineage' to be born in the caste of bangle makers. They have accepted everything as destiny. Years of back-breaking toil have numbed their senses, their desire and courage to dream. But Mukesh is determined to break free from the vicious circle of poverty and start a new life by daring to dream of becoming a motor mechanic.

Understanding the text   (Page 20)

Question 1. What could be some of the reasons for the migration of people from village to cities?

Answer The people are forced to migrate to cities from their villages in search of food and livelihood. The perpetual poverty which exists in their home town forces them to take shelter elsewhere where at least they can have two square meals a day.

Question 2. Would you agree that promises made to poor children are rarely kept? Why do you think this happens in the incidents narrated in the text?

Answer   Yes, I agree that promises made to poor children are rarely kept. It is mostly the rich and people belonging to affluent classes who indulge in making false promises to innocent children. These promises are a bait in some cases. In others, they are meant to avoid these children because they are a nuisance for most people. If, in case, any individual stops to hear their unfortunate saga of life, it is only because of sympathy, a means of giving suggestion or encouragement.

Most people, like the author, do this because they feel, somewhere, it kindless a hope in the hearts of these children of a lesser God. When the author, Anees Jung, asks Saheb about school, his matter-of-fact reply that there is no school, forces her to say casually that she will build one. What the author does not realise is the fact that though she only feels embarrassed at her false promise, it can have a deep impact on the child. Later in life, Saheb may never actually believe, the promises made by people. Moreover, he may feel disappointed and thereby start believing that—Promises are meant to be broken.

Question 3. What forces conspire to keep the workers in the bangles industry of Firozabad in poverty?

Answer   Firozabad is the hub of India's glass-blowing industry where families have spent generations making bangles to adorn married women. The stark reality of these families is that inspite of the back-breaking hardwork they put in, they cannot have two square meals a day. They work in deplorable conditions and many lose their eyesight early. To top it all, they live in unhygenic conditions where there is a lack of basic amenities too.

The sad reality is that the workers cannot organise themselves into a co-operative. They are devoid of all enthusiasm and do not dare to dream. Many believe, like Mukesh's grandmother, that a god-given lineage cannot be altered and thus, have accepted their fate. The fear of police, lack of leadership among themselves have really pulled them down. They are caught in a vicious circle of poverty, indifference and greed.

There are basically two forces that have conspired to keep them backward, firstly, their birth in a poverty stricken family where they received the art of bangle making as a heritage. Secondly, they are caught in a hopeless situation, where there is a nexus between the politicians, the sahukars, the middlemen, police and unwieldy, power-hungry bureaucrats. Still the author feels children like Mukesh can rewrite their fate and alter their destiny.

Talking about the text   (Page 20)

Question 1. How, in your opinion, can Mukesh realise his dream?

Answer   Mukesh belongs to a family of bangle-makers, but his attitude to his situation is different from that of other family members. He dreams of becoming a motor-mechanic and learning to drive a car. His determination for becoming a motor-mechanic and learning to drive a car seems to be very strong.

That is why he says that he will walk to the garage. There he will have to meet the owner of the garage and request him for any petty work pertaining to the garage.

Through his sincere efforts and hard work and the guidance of his owner, he can attain the skills of a mechanic and then gradually that of car driving. In this way, he can surely realise his dream.

Question 2. Mention the hazards of working in the glass bangles industry.

Answer   It's almost like a tradition in Firozabad to work in the glass bangles industry, even after knowing the parameters of legal section which clearly states that working of children in such industries is illegal at such a tender stage, thousands of children are employed as bangle makers in this industry. They sit with their parents and work in the glass furnaces in dingy cells burning with temperature. Although there are many unseen hazards of working in the glass industry but the one which has a direct impact is on the eye sight. The eyes are more adjusted to the dark than the light outside. This is the reason which often leads to loss of eyesight even before the children become adults. Mukesh's grandfather also became blind due to the dust while polishing the glass bangles. Such kind of vigorous and continued labour has impaired the ability to dream of thousands of boys and girls.

Question 3. Why should child labour be eliminated and how?

Answer   Child labour should be eliminated completely because it reflects the condition of the nation. Childhood which is a tender age to receive love and care should not be spent in working and that too in such life threatening conditions. It is a matter of great grief and concern that India has the maximum number of child workers. Across India all major industries employ a large number of child workers because they are considered to be swift workers.

Apart from the bangles industry in Firozabad, carpet industry in Mirzapur and fireworks factory in Sivasaki are others in the line following such shameful activity of child labour. Just to maximize ones own profit people are forgetting that they are curbing the growth of the nation because children are our future. Child labour is absolutely illegal; therefore strict action should be taken against those who are employing children in such hazardous industries. The guilty should be punished immediately. In view with the present condition, it is only exemplary punishment that can put a control over such practice.

Thinking about language   (Page 20)

Carefully read the following phrases and sentences taken from the text. Can you identify the literary device in each example?

1. Saheb-e-Alam which means the lord of the universe is directly in contrast to what Saheb is in reality.
2. Drowned in an air of desolation.
3. Seemapuri, a place on the periphery of Delhi yet miles away from it, metaphorically.
4. For the children it is wrapped in wonder; for the elders it is a means of survival.
5. As her hands move mechanically like the tongs of a machine, I wonder if she knows the sanctity of the bangles she helps make.
6. She still has bangles on her wrist, but not light in her eyes.
7. Few airplanes fly over Firozabad.
8. Web of poverty.
9. Scrounging for gold.
10. And survival in Seemapuri means rag-picking. Through the years, it has acquired the proportions of fine art.
11. The steel canister seems heavier than the plastic bag he would carry so lightly over his shoulders.

Answers

1. Hyperbole	2. Metaphor	3. Contrast
4. Contrast	5. Simile	6. Contrast
7. Contrast	8. Metaphor	9. Hyperbole
10. Hyperbole	11. Contrast	

3

Deep Water

William Douglas

Introduction

William Douglas was born in Maine, Minnesota in 1898. He spent two years teaching in high school in Yakima after graduating with Bachelors of Arts in English and Economics. When tired of teaching, he pursued a legal career. He met Franklin D Roosevelt and became an advisor and a friend to the President. He was the longest serving Justice as his term lasted thirty-six years. The following excerpt is taken from 'Of Men aznd Mountains' by William O' Douglas. It is an autobiographical part revealing how he overcame his fear of water.

The Story Retold

Talks about a childhood incident; decides to learn swimming

The author remembers the incident which happened when he was ten or eleven years old. He had decided to learn swimming at the YMCA pool at Yakima. His mother had often warned him of the dangers of the Yakima river which she said was very treacherous as many cases of drowning had taken place in the river. The author considered the pool safe as it was nine feet deep and two or three feet at the shallow end. Also, the drop was gradual. The author was conscious of his skinny legs and hated the idea of walking naked into the pool but he subdued his pride and decided to pursue his intentions.

Narrator's aversion for water bodies

From a very young age, the author had developed a hatred for water because of an incident which had happened when he was three or four years old. He had gone to California beach with his father where he was swept over by a wave. His father had only laughed at it but the incident had left terror in the narrator's heart.

Begins to feel comfortable in water

The sight of the pool reminded him of his childhood experience. He somehow mustered courage and paddled with his new water wings. He tried to ape others while trying hard to learn swimming. After two or three days, just as he had been feeling comfortable with the sport, a misadventure happened with him at the pool.

The misadventure in the pool; strategy to manage crisis

The narrator went to the pool when no one was there. The water in the pool was clear. He felt timid about going alone into the pool, so he waited for the others. Just then a boy of good physical built who must have been about eighteen walked in. He had thick hair on his chest and rippling muscles. He yelled and said, "Hi, Skinny, How'd you like to be ducked?". He picked up the author and threw him into the pool. The narrator landed in the water in a sitting position. He swallowed water while moving down. Though he was frightened, yet he had not lost his wits. On his way down, he planned to spring back to the surface as his feet touched the bottom.

Scenario at the bottom of the pool

The way down took longer than what he had imagined. His lungs were about to burst but he accumulated all his strength and made a spring upwards. He came up slower than he had expected. When he opened his eyes he saw nothing but water which had a dirty yellow tinge. This frightened him. He tried to clutch the rope at the side of the pool but only water came in his hand. He tried to yell and shout but no sound came out. Only his eyes and nose came out of the water not his mouth.

The narrator's futile efforts to survive

He swallowed more water and almost choked. His legs hung dead, almost paralyzed. He felt a great force pulling him down. He again started on his long journey down. He tried putting in all his strength as in a nightmare. His lungs ached and he felt dizzy. Yet he remembered his strategy of jumping back to the surface, and moving to the edge of the pool to safety.

Terrified; makes another attempt to rescue himself

He felt himself going down endlessly. When he opened his eyes he saw only darkness through which nothing could be seen. He was struck with terror on which he had no control. Only a person who himself has experienced it can understand this. He was shouting under water but he only felt stiff and rigid. Only his throbbing heart made him aware of being alive. Suddenly he experienced reason which reminded him that he touched the bottom. When he felt the tiles of floor under him, he again jumped up with all his might. This made no difference as he found himself still in water. Terror started gripping him more and more. He trembled, his arms and legs wouldn't move. He tried calling out for his mother.

The narrator gets rescued

Suddenly he felt there was light. He felt that he was coming out of water. His nose was almost out of water when he felt himself going down the third time. He tried sucking air but only swallowed more water. All his efforts ceased, he felt a blackness sweeping over his brain which wiped away his fear and terror. Everything was quiet and peaceful. He felt as if he was in the tender arms of his mother. Then he fell into forgetfulness.

Psychological affect of fear; develops phobia for water bodies

Next what he remembered was lying on his stomach and vomiting. The boy who had thrown him in the pool was panic-stricken and said that he had only been fooling around. Several hours later he walked back home. He felt weak and that night he cried. For days that followed, he was still gripped with a haunting fear. He never went to the pool after that.

After some years; the fear returns

A few years later, when he heard of the waters of the Cascades, he felt like getting into it. Whenever he was in water, whether wading or bathing, he was seized with terror. This handicap carried on even when years passed by ruining all his fishing, boating or swimming trips, depriving him of all joy.

Determines to get rid of the fear

The author tried his best to overcome his fear. Finally, one October he decided to get an instructor to learn swimming. He went to the pool and practiced five days a week, an hour each day. The instructor put a belt around the narrator. A rope was attached to the belt and he practiced forward and backward. Hour after hour, day after day, week after week, he practiced. Amidst each trip across the pool, a bit of panic seized him. It was almost three months before the tension slackened. The instructor taught him to put his face under water and exhale, to raise his nose and inhale. He was made to repeat this exercise hundreds of times. Slowly and steadily, the author was able to shed the fear of his. For weeks, he was made to kick with his legs. Initially, his legs were stiff but gradually they relaxed and he could command them.

Next the instructor, piece by piece, perfected each part and then put it together. In April, he was able to swim, dive etc. Thus, the instructor was relieved.

Strenuous practice gives good results

The author wanted to confirm whether he would be terror-stricken if he was alone. Every time he went to the pool, he would say to terror, "Trying to scare me, eh? Well, here's to you! Look!" after which he would do another length of the pool.

This practice carried on till July. He was still not satisfied so he decided to go to Lake Wentworth in New Hampshire, there only once did the terror return, when he was swimming and was in the middle of the lake. He was able to overcome his terror. He chided himself by saying, "Well, Mr Terror, what do you think you can do to me?"

Still the author had some doubts. At the first opportunity, he hurried west and went to Tieton to Conrad Meadows, up the Conrad Creek Trail to Meade Glacier. He camped himself in the high meadow. Next morning he swam across the Warm Lake just as Doug Corpron used to do. He was thrilled and shouted with joy. He had conquered his fear of water.

The experience enriched the author as a human being

The narrator felt triumphed that he had finally conquered his paralysing fear. He says that death is full of peace but the fear of death terrorizes and makes one lose one's peace of mind. He vividly recalls Roosevelt's words to justify his condition. He says, "All we have to fear is fear itself". His brush with death and the haunting fear of death intensified his will to live.

Thus, the essay potrays a real life personal account of experiencing fear and the steps taken to overcome it. It is a psychological analysis of fear which makes us realise the value of perseverance and patience in tackling fear.

Exercises

Think as you read (Page 27)

Question 1. What is the 'misadventure' that William Douglas speaks about.

Answer William Douglas, the narrator recounts a terrifying childhood experience when he came face to face with death. When he was ten or eleven years old, Douglas was tossed into a 9 feet deep swimming pool at YMCA by a bigger boy just for the sake of 'fooling'. Although he was a beginner, Douglas did not lose heart and planned to push himself up with all his force. He thought once he comes to the surface, he would paddle to the edge of the pool.

Unfortunately, this strategy did not work. He could not pop out of the water like a cork. His legs failed to support him. Terror gripped him with water all around him, he did not know what to do. His lungs were ready to burst out and the pounding heart with throbbing head made things worse. He couldn't scream and was frozen with fear. He was breathless and instead of air sucked water. It seemed that the water around him was still and no amount of effort helped him. All around him there was a mass of yellow water. Suddenly, he felt there were tender arms around him and he was rescued.

Question 2. What were the series of emotions and fears that Douglas experienced when he was thrown into the pool? What plans did he make to come to the surface?

Answer When Douglas was thrown into the pool, he was very much scared but he did not lose his mind. He planned that he would make a big jump when his feet would touch the bottom. Thus, he would come to the surface. Unfortunately, the plan failed. Douglas then grew panicky and started suffocating. He felt that he would die, and then he lost consciousness.

Question 3. How did this experience affect him?

Answer After being rescued, Douglas had lost consciousness and found himself beside the pool lying on his stomach and vomitting. This misadventure left him weak and trembling. He shook fiercely and cried at night. He couldn't eat anything and for days a haunting fear was lurking in his heart. The slightest exertion troubled him, making him weak in the knees and sick in his stomach. He feared water and avoided it.

Think as you read   (Page 29)

Question 1. Why was Douglas determined to get over his fear to water?

Answer After some years, Douglas desperately wanted to get rid of his paralysing fear because any activity, be it wading or bathing, in the water would bring back the icy horror of the pool. It was a terrible handicap that had seized his mind completely. He was being obssessed with it. His legs would become paralysed thinking of the swimming pool incident.

He wanted to overcome it because the agonising fear had ruined his fishing trips and deprived him of the joy of canoeing, boating and swimming.

Question 2. How did the instructor "build a swimmer" out of Douglas?

Answer Douglas' agonising fear was ruining his life. He could not enjoy even the day to day activities related to water sports. Finally, he decided to get an instructor and learn to swim. The instructor understood the magnitude and severity of the terror that gripped him. So, he built a swimmer piece by piece. Firstly, the instructor put a belt around his waist and attached it to a pulley that ran on an overhead cable. For three months, Douglas was repeatedly made to go back and forth across the pool.

Then, Douglas was taught to put his face under water and exhale and to raise his nose and inhale. Bit bit, the narrator was able to shed his panic that seized him when his head was under water.

Later, for weeks together, he was made to kick with his legs at the side of pool. At first, his legs refused to command him but gradually with practice, he could manage his legs. Then, the instructor built a swimmer bit by bit and put each bit together into an integrated whole. Finally, he told the narrator to swim which the narrator managed to do quite successfully.

Question 3. How did Douglas make sure that he had conquered the old terror?

Answer After the instructor completed his training, Douglas wanted to cross check if he had really conquered his old terror. So, he tried swimming all alone in the pool. Only a slight trace of terror would return which he managed to tackle well. He would go for another length of the pool by chiding his fear, "Trying to scare me, eh? Well, here's to you! Look!"

Still not satisfied, Douglas went to Lake Wentworth and swam there practising all the strokes. Only once he felt that the old terror returned. When he put his face under the water, he felt the old sensation return. He conquered it light heartedly and it fled.

Douglas didn't want the slightest traces of fear to remain. So he went west and camped besides the Warm Lake. He dived into the lake and only when he swam across to the other shore and back, he shouted with joy. Finally, he was sure that he had defeated his old ally-the phobia of water bodies.

Understanding the text   (Page 29)

Question 1. How does Douglas make clear to the reader the sense of panic that gripped him as he almost drowned? Describe the details that have made the description vivid?

Answer Douglas mentions each and every detail vividly. Although panicky, he had his strategy in place- popping up like a cork and then paddling to the edge of the pool. Unfortunately, his first attempt failed and terror seized him.

He tried to grab a rope but his hands clutched only at water. He was suffocating and tried to yell but no sound came out. His legs were paralysed, lungs ached and head throbbed. He was dizzy and trembled with fright. His voice was frozen. The only signs of life in him were his beating heart and pounding head.

Douglas tried to strike back by jumping hard. This did not make a difference as there was water all around. He attempted to come out of water a third time, but in vain. He sucked for air and got water. Finally, he stopped making efforts and fainted into oblivion.

All the above details of his gripping, near drowning experience make us feel that we are experiencing his lurking terror step by step. The clarity with which he explains is amazing and makes the reader visualise his dismal condition aptly.

Question 2. How did Douglas overcome his fear of water?

Answer Refer to Question 3 Think as you read (Page 23)

Question 3. Why does Douglas as an adult recount a childhood experience of terror and his conquering of it? What larger meaning does he draw from this experience?

Answer Douglas as an adult recounts his childhood experience of terror and his ability to conquer it to portray that nothing is impossible when a person wants to set things possible. Determination is the only thing required to overcome any hurdle in life. He faced this thing practically when a big bully tossed him into the deep end of the YMCA pool. At that moment, he felt tensed and suffocated. His legs became rigid, his lungs ached and heart throbbed. Then, stark terror took him into oblivion. When he regained senses, he found himself lying beside the pool.

Thorough training from an instructor finally made him a swimmer, but old signs of fear would still disturb. Then, he went to Lake Wentworth and dived off a dock. He swam two miles across the lake. At last, he was able to conquer his fear of water. For Douglas, this was not just a simple experience but life changing and transforming. He feared death and had experienced the sensation of dying through this particular experience but when he overcame his fear through persistent efforts, he found himself as a new person who was more positive and determined now. His experience serves as a useful lesson to all the readers to fight bravely in all kind of circumstances. This has been well illustrated by Roosevelt who states; "All we have to fear is fear itself".

Talking about the text   (Page 30)

Question 1. "All we have to fear is the fear itself". Have you ever had a fear that you have now overcome? Share your experience with your partner.

Answer   Fear is just a state of mind. If we dread things they become difficult and unattainable and the moment we get determined to overcome from a particular fear every hurdle resolves. Almost everyone has a fear through which they live. It depends upon us whether we want to dwell on it or break the barriers and live life as a better person.

Like Douglas who had the fear for deep water, I had the fear from height. Whenever I used to get on some height I used to feel that I will fall and die. Tall buildings and hill stations were something I used to keep myself away from. My fear had crossed all the limits when one day I climbed a ladder to pull something down and I felt as this was the end of world for me. Finally it was my mother who came to my rescue and helped me to overcome my fear from height. A holiday was planned for me to Gantok, so that I could experience the beauty of height. Things have a different perception when looked from above. There my parents made me climb a particular mountain. As I kept climbing up my fears soared, but when I finally reached the top and looked below, things started looking beautiful as never before. From that point, I overcame my greatest fear and feel myself to be a better and relaxed person.

4

The Rattrap

Selma Lagerlöf

Introduction

'The Rattrap' is a story that gives us a psychological insight into human nature. Set amidst the mines of Sweden, the author highlights how greed and avarice for material things entrap human beings into this world. He reaffirms our faith in the essential goodness in a human being that can be awakened through understanding and love.

The Story Retold

About the vagabond

The story is about a poor wanderer who went around selling small rattraps to make both ends meet. He used to beg even for the material used for making rattraps. It was difficult to make a living out of rattraps so he resorted to begging and petty thefts.

The vagabond's thought about the world

One day when he was lonely, he became engrossed in his own thoughts. He mused on the thought that the whole world is a big rattrap. All the comforts and the joys it offers are nothing but baits to entrap people. The vagabond strongly feels that as soon as we yield to the temptations being offered by the world it spells doom for us.

The intimate host; makes the vagabond his confidant

One dark evening as he was walking along the road, he sought shelter in a small gray cottage by the roadside. The owner of the cottage was an old man, without a wife or children. He happily accommodated him and offered him food. A kind hearted soul, the host confides in the vagabond that he was formerly a crofter at Ramsjo Ironworks. He now earned his living by milking a cow. He had earned thirty kronor by selling the milk last month. He also shows the money to the vagabond that was kept in a pouch hung on a nail near the window frame.

The vagabond steals the money

The guest, *i.e.*, the vagabond thanked the host for his generosity and went his own way. The old man locks his house and goes to milk the cow. After half an hour, the guest returned again, smashed the window pane and stole the money. He decided that after committing the theft it would not be safe for him to continue on the highway. So he turns off the road, into the woods.

The vagabond gets lost in the woods

He walks through a labyrinth of different paths in the "big and confusing" forest. He soon realises that he had only been walking "around in the same path of the forest". He is tired beyond measure and the thoughts about the world being a rattrap re-occur in his mind. He realises that the whole forest is "like an impenetrable prison from which he would never escape".

The wanderer reaches Ramsjo Ironworks

The vagabond saw no hope of coming out of the dense forest so he felt dejected and tired. As he laid his head on the ground, he heard the sound of regular thumping of a hammer. He realises that an iron mill is somewhere in the vicinity. He gathered all his strength and walked in the direction of the sound.

He reaches Ramsjo Ironworks where the mastersmith and his helper sat in the dark forge near the furnace. One could feel that the work was going on in full swing and many sounds could be heard in the forge.

The vagabond creeps into the iron mill

The vagabond opened the gate and entered the forge in search of shelter on that cold and rainy December night. He sought permission from the master blacksmith to stay overnight. He was granted permission haughtily. The vagabond slept close to the furnace in order to warm himself.

The ironmaster's routine nightly visit

The owner of the mill was particular about the quality of iron that was sent into the market. That night he came to the mill on his round of inspection. The presence of the vagabond lying there caught his attention. He looked at him closely and mistook him for captain Nils Olof, a close colleague of his belonging to the same regiment. The vagabond does not disclose his real identity thinking that he could get some money from the ironmaster. The ironmaster invites him to his manor house.

The wayfarer declines his invitation

The wanderer is alarmed at the very thought of going to the manor house because the thirty kronor that he has stolen could put him into a tight spot. So, he deliberately and firmly rejects the ironmaster's offer. The ironmaster assumes that probably the captain is embarrassed of his ragged and miserable clothes. He tries to mitigate his fears by telling him that he stays with his oldest daughter here and so it won't be embarrassing at all to come to his place. All his sons are settled abroad and his wife Elizabeth is dead. The ironmaster says both of them will enjoy his company on the Christmas Eve. The tramp's constant refusals, finally, make him give in and he goes away.

Ironmaster sends daughter to pursue the tramp

After about half an hour, the daughter of the ironmaster arrives. She was not pretty but quite modest and shy. As she approaches him, the tramp is quite alarmed and frightened. She introduces herself as Edla Willmansson and requests him to stay with them for the Christmas Eve. She says that he could leave after Christmas anytime.

The tramp changes his mind

The rattrap peddler gives in to her request and covers himself with the fur coat carried by the lady's valet. On the way, he feels guilty for stealing the money. He finds himself completely entrapped. He is sure that he cannot come out of it.

The ironmaster's and his daughter's views about the guest

The ironmaster wishes that his 'old regimental comrade' should become healthy. He should do something better than selling rattraps. His daughter is surprised that the captain's condition has become so dismal. She says that she did not find anything in the guest that pointed out that he was an educated man.

The father asks his daughter to be patient and wait till the time the guest sheds his tramp manners and gets groomed.

The ironmaster does not find resemblance between the guest and his comrade

The ironmaster realises that the guest did not resemble his colleague of the regiment even after being well-dressed. He is not pleased and demands explanation about the events from the stranger. The tramp says that he never pretended to be what he is not. He had only come to the forge seeking shelter. He offers to remove the clothes, put on his rags and go away from there.

However, the ironmaster says that his behaviour has not been honest. He hints at taking the matter to the Sheriff.

The tramp's explanation; ironmaster's view

The tramp is really agitated at this and hits the table with his fist. He says that the whole world is a rattrap. All good things in life are a bait used to entrap us. He says that the ironmaster is not impeccable or flawless himself. Someday, it is possible that he might be tempted too and entrapped in the ways of the world.

The ironmaster is convinced by his argument and says that he will not get the Sheriff to intervene in the matter. He asks the tramp to leave immediately.

Edla insists on his staying back for Christmas

At this Edla wishes that the tramp stays back. She feels that it will be wrong to send him away after promising Christmas cheer. She feels that the unwanted, taken-for-granted man deserves a better deal. The father gives in. However, the vagabond cannot gauge her motive behind the kind treatment being meted out to him.

The Christmas Eve and the tramp

After sharing the Christmas fare, the stranger sleeps the whole afternoon. In the evening, he comes downstairs when the Christmas tree is lighted, stood there for a while and then again sleeps for two hours. Finally, he is awakened to eat the Christmas fish and porridge.

After the Christmas dinner, he thanks and wishes good night to everyone present. The ironmaster's daughter is still very kind towards him and says that he can keep her father's suit as a Christmas gift. She welcomes him back to spend the next Christmas Eve with them. The tramp is really amazed at her words.

The morning after Christmas; Edla opens the package

Leaving behind the sleeping tramp, the father and daughter go off to the Church, In the Church, they get to know about the theft.

They return home. The girl is very dejected to hear about the theft. The ironmaster is unhappy that he let the tramp into his house. He is sure that the tramp must have disappeared by now with their silverware. However, he is informed by the valet that the stranger had gone empty handed and left behind a Christmas present for Edla. Edla opens up the badly-packaged gift and "gave a little cry of joy". She found a small rattrap and three wrinkled kronor notes that the tramp had stolen from the old man.

The tramp's letter

The tramp was overwhelmed with gratitude for Edla's behaviour towards him and her captain like treatment given to him. He says that he wants to reciprocate the gesture in a dignified way. The peddler asks her to return the thirty kronor to the old man and gifts her a small rattrap. He also writes a letter to her thanking her for elevating him to the status of a captain. He says, this act of hers has transformed him for the better. This is the reason why he has left his old ways. He signs his name as captain Von Stahle because this name gave him the power to clear his conscience.

Exercises

Think as you read   (Page 34)

Question 1. From where did the peddler get the idea of the world being a rattrap?

Answer The peddler was a very poor man who earned his living by selling the rattraps, he made himself from the materials he got by begging. His mind, thus, was always preoccupied with rattraps. Suddenly he thought of the whole world as a big rattrap. The shelter, food, clothes, riches and joys that the world provides are all baits to entrap men. When one is trapped, everything comes to an end.

Question 2. Why was the tramp amused by this idea?

Answer The world had never been kind to the peddler. So he was full of bitterness against the world. He had become a cynic and he enjoyed visualizing the world as a rattrap ready to entrap anybody who was tempted by the baits it had to offer. He knew that many people had been ensnared and the others were still circling around the bait.

Question 3. Did the peddler expect the kind of hospitality that he received from the crofter?

Answer The peddler had never been treated kindly by the world. He was meted out a cold treatment wherever he went. He was pleasantly surprised when the crofter greeted him with warmth and hospitality. Ordinarily he always met 'sour faces' when he knocked for shelter and food.

Question 4. Why was the crofter so talkative and friendly with the peddler?

Answer The old crofter was lonely and leading a dreary existence as he had no wife or children. The old man was happy to get someone to talk to, even though it was a tramp. So, he welcomed the peddler and extended his hospitality towards him.

Question 5. Why did the crofter show the thirty kronor to the peddler?

Answer The crofter had nobody to share his happiness with. He was really satisfied and overjoyed to earn thirty kronor in a month. Hence, he showed the amount to the peddler. Another possible reason is that he suspected that his guest did not believe him.

Question 6. Did the peddler respect the confidence reposed in him by the crofter?

Answer The peddler found it difficult to make both ends meet. His life was enveloped in bitter struggles for mere survival. So, the moment he gets to know about the thirty kronor, he is on an lookout to grab them. Finally he steals the money by smashing a window pane and hows no regard for the crofter's faith,

Think as you read   (Page 37)

Question 1. What made me peddler think that he had indeed fallen into a rattrap?

Answer After grabbing the money from the crofter's, the peddler is cautious enough to avoid the public highway. He gets into the woods but finally realises that it is a big and confusing forest. The end of the forest is no where in sight. He feels he has come to a dead end as he has been walking around the same part of the forest. That's when he recalls his thoughts about the world being a rattrap and he realises that he had indeed fallen into a rattrap.

Question 2. Why did the ironmaster speak kindly to the peddler and invite him home?

Answer In the glow of the furnace, the ironmaster mistook the peddler to be Nils Olof, his old regimental comrade. He was overwhelmed with sympathy for his comrade when he saw him in the terrible condition. The ironmaster wanted the peddler to shed his inhibitions and enjoy on the occasion of Christmas. Moreover, the ironmaster wanted to better his comrade's future prospects.

Question 3. Why did the peddler decline the invitation?

Answer The peddler did not disclose his real identity and did not make an effort to clear the ironmaster's misconception. This is because he thought he might get some money in the bargain. But he had to decline the invitation because he feared getting caught as he had stolen the thirty kroner. To go up to the manor house would be like 'throwing, himself voluntarily into the lion's den'.

Think as you read   (Page 41)

Question 1. What made the peddler accept Edla Willmansson's invitation?

Answer The peddler was taken in by Edla's compassion and friendly behaviour. He felt confidence in her when she said, "you will be allowed to leave us just as freely as you came". Thus, the warmth and sincerity shown by the ironmaster's daughter mitigated all his fears.

Question 2. What doubts did Edla have about the peddler?

Answer Although young, Edla was better judge of human character as compared to her father. When she invited the peddler to the manor house, she concluded immediately that he had either stolen some money or had escaped from the jail. She observed that he hardly looked educated.

Question 3. When did the ironmaster realise his mistake?

Answer The ironmaster brought the tramp to his house mistaking him to be his old regimental comrade. However, it was not so. The ironmaster realised this when the valet had given the peddler a bath, a shave, a hair cut and fine clothes. When he was brought before the ironmaster in broad daylight, he understood that he had mistaken the tramp to be his former comrade in the light of the furnace.

Question 4. What did the peddler say in his defence when it was clear that he was not the person the ironmaster had thought he was?

Answer The peddler told the ironmaster that he never pretended to be the captain. Moreover, he did not accept the ironmaster's invitation to come to the manor house. Infact, he had implored him to stay that night in the forge itself.

Question 5. Why did Edla still entertain the peddler even after she knew the truth about him?

Answer A compassionate girl, a true Christain, Edla could not bear the thought of a poor wretch been turned out of the house on the eve of Christmas. She is pained at the idea that everybody chases the vagabond away. So, she wanted that the peddler should "enjoy a day of peace with us here just one in the whole year".

Think as you read (Page 42)

Question 1. Why was Edla happy to see the gift left by the peddler?

Answer Edla became happy after seeing the gift of the peddler because 'the gift' proved her father's rigid belief that the peddler was a thief and nothing, including her belief in the better part of human being, could change him. However, 'the gift' proved that her 'belief' was right, so she felt immense joy.

Question 2. Why did the peddler sign himself as Captain Von Stahle?

Answer The peddler owed his transformation to the kind treatment meted out to him by Edla. Inspite of knowing his antecedents, she had honoured and treated him like a captain. She had awakened the latent goodness in his heart. It is because of her that he could clear his conscience. He would have remained a petty thief had he not been elevated to the rank of a captain.

Understanding the text (Page 43)

Question 1. How does the peddler interpret the acts of kindness and hospitality shown by the crofter, the ironmaster and his daughter?

Answer Initially, the peddler seems to be a man who has no principles in life. He heartily accepts the crofter's hospitality and generosity but robs him of his hard-earned kronor just because it is easy to get it. He hardly cares for the faith reposed in him by the old man.

When the ironmaster mistakes him to be his old regimental comrade, he does not disclose his true identity in the hope of getting a few kronor. However, when the ironmaster pesters him he feels a sense of entrapment, having stolen the money from the crofter's and declines the invitation. He feels that to accept the invitation would be like voluntarily throwing himself into the lion's den. He only wants to stay for a night in the forge and slip out in the morning. However, on Edla's invitation he does go there. When the ironmaster realises his mistake, the peddler acts in ungrateful manner and gives him a 'sermon' about the whole world being a rattrap.

Edla's warmth, sympathy and hospitality transform him in the end. Her elevating him to the status of a captain makes him redeem himself from a petty thief. It stirs the innate goodness of his heart. Edla truly believes him and the tramp repays her faith in him by leaving behind the stolen kronor to be returned to the crofter. He also leaves behind a small rattrap as a Christmas gift and thanks her whole-heartedly. He says that having been treated with such respect, he could not hope to embarrass them. He had been saved from the dubious fate of being caught in the rattrap of the world for which he was indebted to her. That's the reason why he signs off as Captain Von Stahle.

Question 2. What are the instances in the story that show that the character of the ironmaster is different from that of his daughter in many ways?

Answer   A man of power and ambition, the ironmaster was in the habit of visiting the forge at night to ensure that good iron was shipped out from his end. When he saw the tramp near the forge, he mistook him to be his old regimental comrade who had fallen into bad times. He wanted to take the man to the manor house, not out of sympathy or philanthropy but out of arrogance. The ironmaster wanted him to realise that resigning from the regiment was a wrong decision and if he (the ironmaster) was there, the comrade would not have been reduced to poverty.

The ironmaster was not a good judge of human character. That's the reason why he felt that the tramp would regain his sophisticated manners after a bath and change of clothes. When he realises that he has been mistaken, he thoughtlessly jumps to the conclusion of reporting the matter to the Sheriff. Again, on learning in the Church about the peddler's theft, he is worried about his own silverware.

On the other hand, Edla, his daughter understands in the beginning itself that either the tramp has stolen something or has escaped from the jail. She was not convinced that he had ever been in the armed forces. Still, she retains her sympathetic attitude towards him and persuades her father to let him stay because it would be unjust to turn him out of the house on the Christmas Eve. She takes the stranger by hand and asks him to eat in spite of her father's unwillingness.

She realises that the tramp was never welcome anywhere and always been chased away by people. She decides that at least for one day of the year, she would make the tramp feel safe, secure and comfortable in her home. Thus, she paves the way for the tramp's transformation and redemption.

Question 3. The story has many instances of unexpected reactions from the characters to others' behaviour. Pick out instances of these surprises.

Answer   In the first instance, the old crofter's gesture of welcoming the tramp for shelter and some food at night is unexpected. Used to sour faces, even the tramp is surprised by his good luck here. The peddler's act of stealing the crofter's hard-earned kronor, indeed, comes as a shock. The way he does it; by smashing the window-pane and breaching the trust is shocking enough.

Then, the peddler's act of seeking refuge in the forge, meeting the ironmaster and the latter mistaking him to be his old regimental comrade comes as a surprise. His invitation to the tramp to come for the Christmas Eve to the manor house leaves one astounded. The peddler's act of accepting Edla's invitation in spite of his guilt feeling about the stolen money and thoughts about entering the lion's den, baffle us. The next surprise is when the peddler left to himself in the manor house has every opportunity to slip out with the valuables. Even the ironmaster expects something like this to happen. However, the tramp goes away leaving behind a small rattrap as a Christmas gift and the thirty kronor to be returned to the rightful owner shocks the reader out of his wits.

The tramp's letter addressed to Edla expressing his gratitude for elevating him to the status of Captain, giving him a chance to free himself from the rattrap of the world and redeeming him also give us a shock.

Thus, the story is replete with instances of unexpected reactions and surprises.

Question 4.   What made the peddler finally change his ways?

Answer   Love, understanding and acceptance are such things which whenever given shows tremendous and noteworthy results. Similar thing happened in the case of the peddler. A mere thief was transformed into a gentleman who not only left behind the thirty kronors he had stolen for the rightful owner, but he also left a Christmas gift for Edla who was the person responsible for transforming the peddler.

It is not that Edla had treated him extraordinarily but the basic goodness shown towards him was quite effective as that was missing in his life. For the first time he was made to feel like a gentleman and not a thief. The feeling was so special to feel that it tempted him to remain so forever. It was just the simple human behaviour and kindness shown by Edla that compelled the peddler to change his ways.

Question 5. How does the metaphor of the rattrap serve to highlight the human predicament?

Answer   Left to his own meditations, the tramp in the course of his wandering, thinks about the whole world as a big rattrap. Just as cheese and pork are baits in the rattrap, similarly the riches, joy, shelter and food that the world offers are baits to entrap and ensnare people.

Being an embittered man, shunned by everybody, these thoughts give 'unwonted joy' to the tramp. A sadistic and a cynic, he thinks of all the people around him who have fallen into the trap.

The musings of the tramp, too, have an iota of truth in them. We are tempted by all the temptations, desires and needs. We go all out to pursue them. In this desire to amass and accumulate more and more, we are entrapped by the world. Just in case we do not get the things we want, we are plunged in despair and gloom. Caught in the rut, we find ourselves incapable of wriggling out of our day-to-day wishes and desires. The more we try to escape, the more we are engulfed into the trap and lose all means of escape.

Question 6. The peddler comes out as a person with subtle sense of humour. How does this serve in lighting the seriousness of the theme of the story and also endear him to us?

Answer The peddler with his subtle sense of humour equates the rattraps he makes to the world which he believes is a huge rattrap, offering baits like comfort, food, shelter and material benefits. One day, the rattrap encloses us and there is no way out. In this way, the peddler consoles himself about his not-so-wordly ways. His thinking in this manner about the world and his sad and melancholy-self endears him to us.

He manages to arouse our sympathy in spite of his theft at the old crofter's place and breaching his trust. Somewhere, he is right because the old man was wrong in trusting a stranger so much. The leather pouch with the kronor is, indeed, a bait. His insistence on staying in the warm forge and refusal to go with the ironmaster evokes pity. We know that somewhere he is feeling guilty of stealing the kronor. When the ironmaster realises his mistakes, the tramp's 'sermon' about the world being a rattrap, temptations and desires, is really humorous as it seems out of context.

The ironmaster's daughter's kind and sympathetic attitude changes him completely. Even she realises his human worth and treats him with dignity. The tramp's final act of returning the token of love by writing a letter, signing off as the captain and returning the stolen money elevates him in our eyes also. This is the beginning of his transformation into a sensitive and courteous human being. This act of his really evokes our empathy, makes him truly humane and thus, endears him to us.

Without the tramp's philosophizing element of the rattrap and his treatment of it in a humorous way, the story would have been seeped in seriousness.

5

Indigo

Louis Fischer

Introduction

The chapter is an excerpt from the author's book 'The Life of Mahatma Gandhi'. It describes a poor farmer's tenacity to make the great leader visit his district, Champaran, to solve the problems of indigo sharecroppers. It highlights the leadership shown by Gandhi to secure justice for oppressed people through convincing arguments and negotiation. He teaches people to fight their own battles and a lesson in self-reliance.

The Story Retold

The incident which lead Gandhiji to urge British departure

The incident occured in 1917. Gandhiji attended the Annual Convention of the Indian National Congress in 1916. About 2,301 delegates and many visitors were present there. A poor skinny peasant approached Gandhiji and wished him to accompany him to Champaran and grapple with the problems of the peasants there. The peasants of Champaran were sharecoppers. The peasant, Rajkumar Shukla was one of them.

He had come to the Congress session to complain about the injustice of the landlord system in Bihar.

The peasant's perseverance pays off

Gandhi told Shukla that he had to visit Cawnpore and some other places. Shukla patiently accompanied him everywhere. When

Gandhiji returned to his ashram in Ahmedabad, Shukla followed him. Finally Gandhiji agreed to accompany him to Champaran after his Calcutta visit.

The visit to Rajendra Prasad's house

Rajendra Prasad was a lawyer of Patna. He later became the President of the Congress party and India. Rajendra Prasad could not be contacted since he was out of town. Rajkumar and Gandhiji were accomodated for a night there.

Gandhiji's visit to Muzaffarpur

Gandhiji wanted to have more information about the conditions prevailing in Champaran. He sent a telegram to Professor JB Kriplani. Kriplani and his students received Gandhiji at the station.

Gandhiji stayed at a government school teacher, Prof Malkani's house which was unusual because it involved harbouring a man who advocated home-rule.

Gandhiji; the Champion of peasants

The peasants came rushing to Muzaffarpur to meet their champion. Gandhiji met the lawyers who briefed him about the situation. They told him about the fee they collected from the sharecroppers. Gandhiji chided them for collecting high fees.

Gandhiji's conclusion

Gandhiji's course of action was to stop going to the law courts. He said that the fear stricken peasants got little help from the courts so they the courts were useless. They needed to be free from fear.

Farmers and indigo

The Champaran district was divided into large estates owned by Englishmen. They compelled their Indian tenants to grow indigo on 15% land. The farmers were deprived of the indigo harvest and the entire production of indigo was to be given as rent.

Impact of the German synthetic indigo

The landlords charged compensation for releasing peasants from the 15% arrangement. Some peasants signed the agreements willingly. Those who resisted, engaged lawyers to resist it. Soon the news of synthetic indigo reached the peasants. They wanted their money back.

Gandhiji's arrival in Champaran

Gandhiji arrived at Champaran. He visited the secretary of the British landlord's association for details on the matter. The secretary refused to divulge any information to him citing the 'outsider' status of Gandhiji. Gandhiji claimed that he was not an outsider.

Gandhiji also contacted the British official, the Commissioner of Tirhut. However, he tried to bully Gandhiji. He advised him to leave Tirhut.

Gandhiji defies Commissioner's orders

Instead of living in compliance with the Commissioner's orders, Gandhiji left for Motihari accompanied by various lawyers. He was greeted at the station by crowds of peasants. He started operating from a house and continued his investigations. He also decided to go and see a peasant who had been maltreated in a nearby village.

Official notice issued to Gandhiji

Gandhiji was ordered to come back. He did so. Thereafter he was served with an official notice to quit Champaran immediately. Gandhiji signed it and wrote that he would disobey the order. He was summoned to appear in the court the next day.

A busy night; peasants' unbridled support to Gandhiji

Gandhiji remained awake the entire night. He wired Rajendra Prasad to come from Bihar with influential friends. He also sent instructions to the ashram and wired a full report to the Viceroy.

The news of Gandhiji being in trouble with the authorities spread fast. Thousands of peasants came to Motihari and demonstrated in front of the courthouse. This was the beginning of their liberation from fear of the British. The officials were powerless and sought Gandhiji's cooperation in regulating the crowd. This was a proof that the British authority was no longer unchallengeable.

Bafflement of the authorities

Seeing the peasants in such strength, the prosecutor wanted the trial to be postponed. They probably wanted to consult their superiors. Gandhiji protested against the delay. He read out a statement pleading guilty. He clarified that he broke the law to render humanitarian and national service. He claimed to have no disrespect for law but greater respect for the voice of his conscience.

The two hour recess at the court; the court reconvened

Gandhiji was asked to furnish bail for two hours. Gandhiji refused to do so which resulted in his getting released without bail. The judge withheld judgement for several days and Gandhiji was allowed to stay free. Prominent lawyers held discussions with Gandhi about what they would do if Gandhiji is sentenced to prison.

Gandhiji influences the lawyers

In the event of Gandhiji's arrest, the lawyers decided to return to their places. Gandhiji asked them, what about injustice to sharecroppers. They consulted among themselves, thought hard and came to the conclusion that if Gandhiji, being a stranger, was ready to go to the prison then they being residents of the adjoining districts, who knew the case so well, should also court arrest. This was the beginning of the victory in the battle of Champaran.

The first triumph of civil disobedience; inquiry conducted

The Lieutenant Governor of the province dropped the case against Gandhiji. This was the first triumph of civil disobedience in modern India. Gandhiji preceded to conduct an inquiry into the grievances of farmers. He wrote testimonies by about ten thousand peasants. The notes were made and documents were collected. The landlords protested vehemently against such an inquiry.

Gandhiji summoned by the Governor; Sir Edward Gait

Gandhiji met his associates and chalked out detailed plans for civil disobedience in case he is imprisoned. He had four interviews with the Lieutenant Governor, who ordered official commission of inquiry into the indigo sharecroppers predicament. The commission consisted of landlords and government officials. Gandhiji was the sole representative of the peasants.

Planters agree to make refunds to the peasants

A lot of evidence was collected against the landlords. They were left with no choice but to agree in principle to refund the money to the peasants. Gandhiji was asked to quote the amount which was illegally and deceitfully extorted from the sharecroppers. The landlords expected him to ask for full amount but Gandhiji demanded just 50%. He approved the landlord's proposal of 25% as refund.

Gandhiji explains his stand

Gandhiji justified his stand by saying that the amount of refund didn't matter. What mattered was that the landlords were obliged to surrender their prestige. This incident had made the peasants courageous. They realised that they had rights. Later events proved that Gandhiji was correct. Within a few years the British planters abandoned their estates which were reverted to the peasants.

Gandhiji dissatisfied with political and economic solutions

Gandhiji wanted to remove the cultural and social backwardness in the villages of Champaran. He sought volunteers for the work. Devadas, Gandhiji's youngest son arrived from the ashram to carry forward the work. Kasturbai taught the ashram rules on personal cleanliness and community sanitation. The health conditions were really worse. Castor oil, quinine and sulphur ointment were used for curing ailments.

Managing the ashram from Champaran

Gandhiji sent instructions by mail and kept a check on ashram's financial accounts. He also kept in mind the ashram's sanitation. He instructed to fill the old laterine trenches and dig the new ones.

The Champaran episode; a turning point in life

Champaran was not an act of defiance against the authorities. It was an attempt to mitigate the sufferings of the masses. It showed that Gandhiji could not be ordered about in his own country. It revealed that Gandhiji's politics was seeped into practical day to day problems of the people. All his efforts were directed towards making a new, free Indian who would liberate India.

A lesson in self-reliance

Gandhiji's devout follower, Charles Freer Andrews came to bid farewell to Gandhiji in Champaran. Gandhiji's lawyer friends wanted to urge Andrews to stay on and support their cause. However, Gandhiji opposed this vehemently. He said that one must rely upon himself to win the battle. It was meaningless to use Andrews because this shows weakness. One would never become independent and overcome hardships in this manner. Thus, the Champaran episode, self-reliance and Indian independence were held together by a common thread.

Thus, the chapter instills us the qualities of self-reliance and independence. There is no point in depending upon others to win our battles. One's patience, perseverance and untiring efforts are bound to pay off one day.

Exercises

Think as you read (Page 47)

Question 1. Strike out what is not true in the following

    (a) Rajkumar Shukla was
        (i) a sharecropper   (ii) a politician
        (iii) delegate   (iv) a landlord

    (b) Rajkumar Shukla was
        (i) poor
        (ii) physically strong
        (iii) illiterate

Answer   (a) (iv) a landlord
         (b) (ii) physically strong

Question 2. Why is Rajkumar Shukla described as being 'resolute'?

Answer   Rajkumar Shukla was an illiterate indigo farmer from Champaran. He had come to invite Gandhiji to visit his district as there was rampant injustice and oppression prevailing there. Gandhiji mentioned about his prior commitments to other parts of India but Shukla accompanied him everywhere. Eventually Shukla's steadfast attitude bore fruit and Gandhiji agreed to his request. After his Calcutta visit, the two of them preceded for Patna.

Question 3. Why do you think the servants thought Gandhi to be another peasant?

Answer   The servants knew that Rajkumar Shukla was a poor farmer who pestered their master to help the indigo sharecroppers. Since Gandhiji accompanied Shukla and was dressed up simply, they mistook him for a peasant. Gandhiji's modesty and unassertiveness also led to the assumption that he was a peasant.

Think as you read (Page 49)

Question 1. List the places that he visited between his first meeting with Shukla and his arrival at Champaran.

Answer   Gandhiji did not visit Champaran immediately because he had prior commitments in other parts of the country. He was expected to visit Cawnpore after which he returned to his ashram near Ahmedabad. It was only after his visit to Calcutta, Patna and Muzzaffarpur that he was able to accompany Shukla to Champaran.

Question 2. What did the peasants pay the British landlords as rent? What did the British now want instead and why? What would be the impact of synthetic indigo on the prices of natural indigo?

Answer The British landlords had entered into a long term contract with the farmers according to which they compelled all tenants to plant 15% of their holdings with indigo. They had to surrender the entire indigo harvest as rent. Since Germany had developed synthetic indigo that had brought an enormous fall in indigo prices, the landlords wished to give up this arrangement. They demanded compensation for releasing the farmer's land.

Think as you read   (Page 51)

Question 1. The events in this part of the text illustrate Gandhiji's method of working. Can you identify some instances of this method and link them to his ideas of *Satyagraha* and non-violence?

Answer Despite the orders from the commissioner to leave Terhut, Gandhi did not leave – "The commissioner", Gandhiji reports, "proceeded to bully me and advised me forthwith to leave Tirhut", but Gandhiji did not defer because he was fighting for the cause of truth that is *Satyagraha.* "Gandhiji signed a receipt for the notice and wrote on it that he would disobey the order."

The event of his going to court proves his method of 'non-violence'. "Their spontaneous demonstration, in thousands, around the courthouse was beginning of their liberation from fear of the British. The officials felt powerless without Gandhiji's co-operation. *He helped them regulate the crowd.*"

Think as you read   (Page 53)

Question 1. Why did Gandhi agree to a settlement of 25% refund to the farmers?

Answer Gandhiji agreed to a settlement of 25% refund to the farmers in order to break the deadlock between the landlords and peasants. For him the amount of the refund was not very important. The fact that the landlords had been obliged to surrender part of the money as well as their prestige gave a moral victory to the farmers. Thus, Gandhiji not only made the landlords accept their dishonesty but also made the farmers learn a lesson in defending their right and courage.

Question 2. How did the episode change the plight of the peasants?

Answer The Champaran episode made the peasants raise their voice against British supremacy and made them aware of their rights. The episode began a massive movement against the social, cultural and economic backwardness of the region. Within a few years, the British planters abandoned their estates, which reverted to the peasants.

Understanding the text   (Page 54)

Question 1. Why do you think Gandhi considered the Champaran episode to be a turning-point in his life?

Answer The Champaran episode began as an attempt to alleviate the distress of poor peasants. Ultimately it proved to be a turning point in Gandhiji's life because it was a loud proclamation that made the British realise that Gandhiji could not be ordered about in his own country. It infused courage to question British authority in the masses and laid the foundation of non-cooperation as a new tool to fight the British tooth and nail.

Question 2. How was Gandhi able to influence the lawyers? Give instances.

Answer Gandhiji's sincerity towards the peasants' cause, convincing argumentation and negotiation throughly influenced the lawyers. He chided them for overcharging the peasants and encouraged them to court arrest for the peasants' noble cause. He rejected their proposal to seek Mr Andrew's help in their battle against Britishers in order to be self-reliant and independent.

Question 3. What was the attitude of the average Indian in smaller localities towards advocates of 'home rule'?

Answer The average Indian in smaller localities were unaware of the British supremacy. This is the reason why they shunned from showing any sympathy to the advocates of 'home rule'. They feared they would invite the wrath of the British rulers if they harboured such supporters.

Question 4. How do you know that ordinary people too contributed to the freedom movement?

Answer Our freedom movement grew in intensity and numbers not only because of the sacrifices and support of prominent names. Ordinary people also played a very important role. The Champaran episode is an illustration in this regard. Many common people like Rajkumar Shukla and countless names like him fought bravely against British suzerainty and contributed to the freedom struggle. At that moment, it required oodles of courage to come out openly in support of Gandhiji. The first battle of civil disobedience in India was won because of support and solidarity of the masses.

6

Poets and Pancakes

Asokamitran

Introduction

'Poets and Pancakes' is a humourous and interesting account of Asokamitran's experiences at Gemini Studios in Madras. It has interesting vignettes of personalities of a film company in the early days of Indian cinema. He vividly brings out some of the eccentricities and infirmities of the characters in a delightful manner. The present chapter is an excerpt from his book 'My Years with Boss'.

The Story Retold

The make-up department of Gemini Studios

The make-up department was in a building which was said to be Robert Clive's erstwhile stable. In the studios, the make-up material with the brand name 'Pancake' was used profusely. All actresses of yesteryears are familiar with it. The author feels that modern actresses may not be aware of its existence.

The author mocks at Robert Clive by saying that during his short life he is said to have lived in a number of residences in Madras. He fought battles and even got married here.

A vivid description of the make-up room

The make-up room looked like a hair-cutting salon. It was crowded with large mirrors and flooded with light. It was not a very pleasing experience to get the make-up done because of the heat from the dazzling lights.

The make-up department and national integration

The department was initially headed by a Bengali. He was succeeded by a Maharashtrian who was assisted by a Dharwar Kannadiga. Then different people belonging to different states occupied the position there. The author points out that all this shows that the make-up department was an ideal specimen of national integration.

The author jokingly tells the readers about the 'skills' of these make-up men. With quite a lot of Pancake and other potions and lotions, they could mar the beauty of any person. However, Asokamitran clarifies by saying that perhaps the hideous crimson coloured make-up was important to look presentable on the screen.

A strict hierarchy in the make-up department

An elaborate division of work marked the make-up department. The chief make-up man dressed up actors in the lead role. His senior assistant looked after the 'second' hero and heroine while the junior assistant took charge of the main comedian. The crowd was managed by the office boy.

The office boy at Gemini Studios

The office boy was not exactly a boy. He was in his early forties. He joined the studio years back and aspired to be a top film star or top screen writer, director or lyric writer. He also wrote poetry. On the days of crowd-shooting, he mixed the make-up material on a large scale and painted faces.

The narrator's work in the studio

The narrator worked in a cubicle. His work was to cut newspaper clippings and store them in files. Everybody thought that his work was next to nothing and so he was continuously lectured by other employees. The office boy often came to his cubicle and gave a vent to his feelings of frustration and irritation. The narrator desperately wished to escape from his continuous tirade and prayed for crowd shooting.

Kothamanglam Subbu

He was the No. 2 at Gemini Studios. According to the office boy, Subbu did not deserve anything because he was neither well educated nor had any exceptional talent. His only virtue was being a Brahmin due to which he got opportunities readily. He was always cheerful. Even a flop film couldn't take away his cheerfulness.

The narrator takes a dig at him by saying that he always needed people to support him. He was ever-loyal to the Chief. Subbu could offer countless solutions to the problems of the producer. The narrator comments that film making was quite simple with a man like Subbu around.

Subbu; the poet

Although he was capable of writing on intricate topics, he wrote poetry for the masses. His success in films overshadowed his literary genius. He composed 'story poems' in folk refrain and diction. He recreated the mood and manner of the Devadasis of the early 20th century.

Subbu; the actor and the sycophant

The narrator mocks at Subbu by saying that the was an amazing actor. Although he played minor roles, he performed them better than the lead actors. He always said nice things about everything and everyone. His house was crowded with acquaintances. He was really close and intimate with the Boss and he had many enemies.

The lawyer in the Story Department of Gemini Studios

The story department comprised of a lawyer and a group of writers and poets besides Subbu. The lawyer was the legal adviser but everybody referred to him as illegal adviser! He had unintentionally brought about a sad end to the career of a talented actress by recording her outburst against the producer. The legal adviser was different from the department as he wore pants and tie. He was close to the Boss and was allowed to produce a film which flopped. The lawyer lost his job when the Boss closed the story department.

Gemini Studios the favourite haunt of intelligentsia

Gemini Studios was a hot favourite among the poets of that time. It has an excellent mess which supplied good coffee almost round the clock. Those were the days when the Congress government had implemented prohibition and people enjoyed their leisure time over a cup of coffee. Almost everybody seemed to have ample leisure time at the studio.

The political ideology at the studio

Most of the people at the studio wore khadi and greatly appreciated Gandhiji. All of them were opposed to Communism and had many misconceptions about it. They thought Communists to be violent with no filial or conjugal feelings.

Studio hosts Frank Buchman's MRA (Moral Re-armament Army)

The MRA, a counter-movement to international Communism visited Madras in 1952. It comprised of 200 people. The narrator had information that the big bosses of Madras played into their hands. The group was criticised by calling it an international circus. The MRA presented two plays, 'Jotham Valley' and 'The Forgotten Factor'. Their sets and costumes were wonderful. The Gemini family comprising of six hundred members saw the plays repeatedly. The Tamil and Madras drama community were really impressed by them. The sunrise and sunset scenes were reproduced in almost all Tamil plays in a similar fashion on the model of 'Jotham Valley'. The narrator feels that hosting the group was a welcome change from their monotonous routine at the studio.

Another visitor at Gemini Studios

Another visitor was soon going to visit the Gemini Studio. The staff did not have the faintest idea about him. He was rumoured to be a poet or editor. The visitor was not connected with any of the famous British publications. However, the guest arrived and the Boss read out a very long speech that did not have much to say about the visitor. When the guest's turn came to address the audience, his accent could not be understood by anybody. His visit remained an "unexplained mystery."

A short story contest organised by 'The Encounter'

The narrator wanted to have an idea about the periodical's credentials before participating in the contest and spending on the postage. He checked at the British Council Library and found out the editor's name was Stephen Spender. He recalled that this was the same editor who was a guest at the Gemini Studios. The writer felt that he had discovered a long lost brother and immediately sent his entry excitedly.

The narrator buys a low-priced book 'The God That Failed'

The narrator bought a copy of a low-priced book 'The God That Failed' released on the 50th anniversary of the Russian Revolution. It was a compilation of six essays by six different authors on Communism. Stephen Spender was one of the contributors. The narrator instantly recalled Stephen Spender's visit to the Gemini Studios. Thus, the mystery was finally resolved.

Exercises

Think as you read (Page 59)

Question 1. What does the writer mean by 'the fiery misery' of those subjected to make-up?

Answer The writer describes the make-up department of Gemini Studios in detail. The make-up room looked like a hair-cutting salon that was crowded with mirrors and flooded with incandescent lights at all angles. When the artists sat there to close every pore on the face with Pancake, the heat and the flashy lights were really unbearable.

Question 2. What is the example of national integration that the author refers to?

Answer The make-up department of Gemini Studios boasted of people belonging to all religions, castes and communities. It was headed by a Bengali and subsequently by a Maharashtrian, an Andhraite, a Christian, a Tamil and an Anglo-Burmese. The writer terms this phenomena in the Gemini Studios as national integration.

Question 3. What work did the 'office boy' do in the Gemini Studios? Why did he join the studios? Why was he disappointed?

Answer The 'office boy' was responsible for the make-up of the players who played the crowd. On the days of crowd-shooting, one could see him mixing his paint in a giant vessel and "slapping it" on the crowd players. He was in his early forties but he had joined the studio years ago in the hope of becoming a star actor or a top screen writer, director or lyric writer.

The 'office boy' had not realised any of his dreams of becoming a star actor or a top screen writer, director or lyric writer. He was also a poet and he deeply felt that his talent was not being recognised. He was doing a job which was much below his actual calibre.

Question 4. Why did the author appear to be doing nothing at the studios?

Answer The author's job involved scanning the various news items and articles that appeared in different newspapers and keeping a record of them. He was always seen at this desk tearing up newspapers. This gave the impression that he was doing next to nothing at the studios.

Think as you read (Page 61)

Question 1. Why was the office boy frustrated? Who did he show his anger on?

Answer The office boy directed all his anger on Kothamangalam Subbu, the number 2 at the Gemini Studios. He was thoroughly convinced that all his woes, ignominy and neglect were due to Subbu. He gave vent to his anger by denigrating and abusing Subbu in the studios.

Question 2. Who was Subbu's principal?

Answer S S Vasan, the founder of the Gemini Studios was Subbu's principal. Subbu seemed to be close and intimate with him. His loyalty to the Boss led everyone to believe that he was a sycophant. He was always seen with the Boss.

Question 3. Subbu is described as a many-sided genius. List form of his special abilities.

Answer Through Kotharnangalam Subbu, Ashokamitran lampoons people who have nothing exceptional or brilliant about them. They have the inherent quality of outwitting others by their presence of mind, flattery and indispensability. The author projects Subbu as a multi-faceted genius. "He was tailor-made for films" and could come out with instant and countless solutions to a problem in one go. He seems to be a versatile man who knew all intricacies of film making.

Subbu was a literary genius and although he was capable of composing poetry in complex and higher forms, he deliberately chose to write for the masses. A talented actor "he never aspired to do the lead roles." Subbu made things really easy for his Boss and become an 'asset' for the Gemini Studios. His flattery put him in the good books of the Boss. Thus, Subbu perfectly enacted many roles. He was a multi-tasker who had mastered every art in the arena of film making and creative writing.

Question 4. Why was the legal adviser referred to as the opposite by others?

Answer The legal adviser was a man of cold logic and was close to the Boss. He was disliked by others. His notoriety and malicious behaviour brought an end to brilliant career of a talented actress. He had never put to use any of his 'legal' skills. Hence, he was referred to as illegal adviser by others.

Question 5. What made the lawyer stand out from the others at Gemini Studios?

Answer In a "crowd of dreamers", the lawyer was a man of cold logic. The Gemini Studios mostly comprised of Gandhiites and Khadiites, but the lawyer had a different political ideology. Moreover, he wore tie and pants, and sometimes a coat which made him stand out in the midst of khadi wearers.

Think as you read   **(Page 64)**

Question 1. Did the people at Gemini Studios have any particular political affiliations?

Answer   The majority of people at Gemini Studios wore khadi and venerated Gandhiji. Beyond that they had not "the faintest affectation" for political thought of any kind. They were vehemently against Communism and called themselves Gandhiites.

Question 2. Why was the Moral Rearmament Army welcomed at the Studios?

Answer   The Moral Rearmament Army was a kind of counter movement to international Communism. They were welcomed at the Gemini Studios because of their aversion to Communism. The Boss, Mr Vasan simply played into their hands. This was because they opposed those who spread unrest and violence among the innocent and the ignorant.

Question 3. Name one example to show that Gemini Studios was influenced by the plays staged by MRA.

Answer   'Jotham Valley' and 'The Forgotten Factor', the two plays put up by the MRA were so impressive that the Gemini family consisting of six hundred people, saw them over and over again. The scene of sunrise and sunset enacted in the plays with a bare stage, a white background curtain and a tune played on the flute were reproduced by Madras and Tamil drama community for years to come.

Question 4. Who was the Boss of Gemini Studios?

Answer   Mr SS Vasan, the founder of Gemini Studios was called 'The Boss'. He was also the editor of the popular Tamil weekly *Ananda Vikatan*. He had a liking for erudite and scholarly people. He seems to be a gullible man who is surrounded by shallow people and sycophants like Subbu and the lawyer.

Question 5. What caused the lack of communication between the Englishman and the people at Gemini Studios?

Answer   In the first instance, nobody knew, anything about the antecedents of the visitor. Mr Vasan, the Boss made a welcome speech in his honour but that did not dispel any doubts or gave clarifications about the visitor. When the visitor spoke nobody could comprehend what he talked about. Moreover, his accent could not be understood by the 'dazed' audience.

Question 6. Why is the Englishman's visit referred to as unexplained mystery?

Answer   The Englishman's visit baffled everybody in the Gemini Studios. They did not know anything about the credentials of the visitor neither could they comprehend anything from his speech. All of them were 'dazed and silent'. They could not understand what was an English poet doing in a film studio which made Tamil films for the masses, who had no taste for English poetry. So, his visit is termed as an unexplained mystery.

Think as you read   (Page 65)

Question 1. Who was me English visitor to the studios?

Answer   The identity of the English visitor was a mystery for all. Nobody was clear about his identity or profession (poet or editor). After many years of the incident, Asokamitran visited the British Council Library to enquire about a Brisith periodical, 'The Encounter'. He wanted to check the antecedents of the periodical for sending the entry to a short story contest. It was then that he discovered that it was Stephen Spender—the editor of 'The Encounter' who had visited the Gemini Studios.

Question 2. How did the author discover who the English visitor to the studios was?

Answer   The identity of the English visitor was revealed to the author only when he read the editor's name in 'The Encounter'. The author knew that once an English poet had visited the studio and it was Stephen Spender who had visited the studios, but his visit was unfortunately a flop.

Question 3. What does 'The God that Failed' refer to?

Answer   'The God that Failed' refers to a book that was a compilation of essays by six eminent essyists. It was a low-priced student edition, an American paperback, that was issued to commemorate the 50th anniversary of the Russian Revolution. It dealt with the authors' disillusionment with Communism.

Understanding the text   (Page 66)

Question 1. The author has used gentle humour to point out human foibles. Pick out instances of this to show how this serves to make the piece interesting?

Answer   'Poets and Pancakes' has instances of gentle humour interspersed in itself. They highlight human foibles without pointing fingers or having malice against anyone. In the beginning itself the author brings into focus Robert Clive's restless nature by saying, "for his brief life and an even briefer stay in Madras, Robert Clive seems to have done a lot of moving, besides fighting some impossible battles.... and marrying a maiden...." The author repeatedly pokes fun at the office boy's bitterness and bragging about his great literary genius which was being wasted. He ridicules the 'virtue' of Subbu being a Brahmin and thus getting better opportunities and exposure. His inefficiency and dependence on others is highlighted by the author's comment, "He always had work for somebody—he could never do things on his own". Subbu's 'creativity' is shown in his knack for offering instant and countless solutions to problems. Subbu's talent for writing poetry is mocked at by Asokamitran when he says,"...though he was certainly capable of more complex and higher forms, he deliberately chose to address his poetry to the masses." His sycophant nature is highlighted when his house is referred to be a permanent residence for many people. Subbu's flattering nature is brought about by the author's question, "....Was it his general demeanour that resembled a sycophant's?"

Another instance of gentle humour is the reference to the lawyer as the 'illegal adviser'. The 'Boss', Mr Vasan's weakness for being seen amongst erudite and scholarly people and the resultant invitations to unknown poets and editors is hilarious. The author's comment on himself that anything at a reduced price attracted his attention makes us laugh at the apparent idiosyncrasies of human nature. Thus, the author showcases humour in every situation and almost every character but this is only meant to make the piece a gripping one.

Question 2. **Why was Kothamangalam Subbu considered number 2 in Gemini Studios?**

Answer Subbu was neither brilliant nor out-of-the-ordinary, but he at had inherent smartness in him that led him to outwit everybody. He was a sycophant and always close and intimate with the Boss. He always had ready and instant solutions for problems and had the knack of getting the work done from others.

Question 3. **How does the author describe the incongruity of an English poet addressing the audience at Gemini Studios?**

Answer The audience could not make any sense of what the poet or editor was speaking. His accent was unintelligible. There was a communication gap between the dazed audience and the even baffled speaker. Nobody could understand the link between the English poet's thrills and travails and the studios which produced Tamil films for the masses who had no sense of English poetry.

Question 4. **What do you understand about the author's literary inclinations from the account?**

Answer The author seems to be an educated young man whose job entails him to keep scanning the newspapers. He is interested in creative writing and so keeps sending his entries to short story writing contests. Reading seems to be his favourite pastime. He buys books even when he is short of money.

7

The Interview

Introduction

'The Interview' is an excerpt from the author's introduction to the *'Penguin Book of Interviews, An Anthology from 1859 to the Present Day'*. The author expresses his views on the interview as a communication genre. The chapter has two parts. The first part deals with the views of eminent people about the commendable and condemnatory aspects of the interview. The latter part reproduces an actual interview of Umberto Eco, who is being interviewed by Mukund Padmanabhan from 'The Hindu'.

The Story Retold

Part I by Christopher Silvester

Background of the interview

Having a history of over 130 years different people have varied opinions about the uses, modes and advantages of interviews. Till now, thousands of celebrities have been interviewed. Every educated person is familiar with it. Some people claim that it is a source of truth while others feel that in practice it is an art.

Opinions about interviews

Many celebrities despise the interview because it is an encroachment on their privacy. It depreciates their personality in a similar manner as depicted in some primitive cultures, where people believed that if someone takes a photographic portrait of somebody then one is stealing that person's soul.

VS Naipaul is of the opinion that interviews injure people as they lose a part of themselves. Lewis Carrol, the creator of 'Alice in Wonderland' was said to have a just 'horror of the interviewer' because he thought he would be treated as a celebrity. His refusals for interviews helped him keep his fans, acquaintances and interviewers at bay. This gave him great satisfaction and amusement. Later he would narrate such experiences with aplomb.

Rudyard Kipling, HG Wells, Saul Bellow's views on interview

Rudyard Kipling vehemently condemned interviews. His wife, Caroline, writes in her diary that her husband refused giving interviews because he considered them immoral, a crime and an assault which is worthy of punishment. According to him, interviews were something vile and cowardly. He neither held the interviewee in esteem nor the interviewer. Although Kipling criticised the interview he had himself interviewed Mark Twain only a few years before this tirade against interviews.

HG Wells, an eminent science fiction writer, frequently gave interviews but in an interview in 1894 referred to 'the interviewing ordeal'. After this comment he interviewed Joseph Stalin, a great Russian revolutionary fourty years later. Saul Bellow felt that interviewers created so much tension and pressure that he felt suffocated. He describes interviews as 'thumbprints on his windpipe'.

Summing up the genre of interviews

Despite its disadvantages, the interview is an excellent medium of communication. Denis Brain gives an elevated position to the interviewer because of his power and influence over the interviewee. He terms the interview as an expressive medium.

Part II An Interview with Umberto Eco

The second part of the chapter is an extract from an interview of Umberto Eco who is being interviewed by Mukund Padmanabhan from 'The Hindu'.

Umberto Eco is a renowned scholar who is known for his ideas on semiotics (the study of signs), literary interpretation and medieval aesthetics. He is also an author who has an array of works ranging from literary fiction, academic texts, essays, children's books and newspaper articles. He rose to prominence with his work 'The Name of the Rose' which sold a staggering 10 million copies.

Eco's views on his philosophical interests and 'interstices'

The interviewer Mukund Padmanabhan, quotes David Lodge (an English novelist) who had expressed astonishment at Umberto Eco's varied and sizeable works. He expresses his surprise by saying that how could one man do all the things that Umberto Eco did. Umberto Eco says that this is a delusive impression about him because he has always been doing the same thing by writing the same philosophical and ethical ideas in different genres.

Eco discloses his secret of producing such voluminous works. He utilises the 'empty spaces' *i.e.*, the shortest gaps between two different works. That's the reason why he has produced so many works. He calls the 'empty spaces' "interstices".

Eco's intimate and playful style

The interviewer, Mukund Padmanabhan, questions him about his personalised style of work which is quite different from the dull and drab style adopted for writing academic works. He asks him if this comes naturally to him or whether he has to make a conscious effort to develop this style.

At this Umberto Eco replies that he learnt this style of writing when he was 22 years of age. At that time he had presented his first Doctoral dissertation in Italy. His Professor was impressed because he had included his trials and errors in it. He had told the story of his research. His Professor published his dissertation as a book which was his way of complimenting his student. Eco understood that he has to adopt the narrative style in his works also. This led him to become a novelist at the ripe age of 50.

At this stage, Umberto Eco recalls his friend, Roland Barthes. Roland Barthes, an essayist, died frustrated because he could not fulfil his wish of being a creative writer. Umberto says that he never felt this frustration as even his essays had a narrative aspect to them. He says that he started writing novels by accident. They catered to his taste for narration.

The phenomenal success of 'The Name of the Rose'

One day when Umberto Eco had nothing to do, he tried his hand at writing a novel. 'The Name of the Rose' made him famous as a novelist although he is an academician with over 40 works in non-fiction.

Most people know Umberto Eco as a novelist but this doesn't please him. He belongs to the academic community and participates in academic conferences. He writes novels only on Sundays. He accepts the fact that by writing fiction he can reach more people. He says, "I cannot expect to have one million readers with stuff on semiotics".

Mukund, the interviewer asks him if he is surprised by the staggering success of the novel, 'The Name of the Rose'. Since the 'The Name of the Rose' is a serious novel that spins a detective yarn at one level and also ventures into metaphysics, theology and medieval history, it is considered as a difficult and serious read.

Umberto Eco says that he is not puzzled by its staggering sales figures. The only people who look at this in disbelief are journalists and publishers. They believe that people like trash and "don't like difficult reading experiences". He applies his own mind to this. He says that after working the whole day he refreshes himself by watching light entertainment programmes like 'Miami Vice' or 'Emergency Room' after dinner. Similarly, everybody likes light reading only to a certain extent. As such serious reading does have the capability to draw people.

The medieval period to which this book belongs to could have played a major role in its success. For Umberto Eco, the success of the book is a mystery. If he had written it ten years earlier or ten years later it might have not been such a remarkable success story.

Exercises

Think as you read (Page 69)

Question 1. What are some of the positive views on interviews?

Answer Interview is a genre that has become a commonplace of journalism within a span of over 130 years. It is an art that brings out truth and gives us vivid impressions of the interviewee. It is an excellent medium of communication.

Question 2. Why do most celebrity writers despise being interviewed?

Answer Most of the celebrities do not like giving interviews because they believe that interviews leave a deprecating effect on them. Writers like V S Naipaul feel wounded by interviews and lose a part of themselves in the process. Some others like Rudyard Kipling condemn interviews as immoral, an offence, a crime and something vile and cowardly. Saul Bellow feels suffocated during interviews.

Question 3. What is the belief in some primitive cultures about being photographed?

Answer Some primitive cultures condemn photography and view it with suspiction. They dislike themselves being photographed for they have a groundless and false fear of their soul being robbed.

Question 4. What do you understand by the expression "thumbprints on his windpipe"?

Answer Saul Bellow compares interviews to 'thumbprints on the windpipe'. This refers to the fact that interviewers make the interviewees feel suffocated and uneasy during the course of an interview. Here, it won't be wrong to mention that interviewers have been compared to strangulators while interviewees are mere victims.

Question 5. Who, in today's world, is our chief source of information about personalities?

Answer Since interviews were invented over 130 years ago this excellent medium of communication has become our chief source of information. As compared to the other sources of information, say biographies, autobiographies and movies to know about personalities, interviews convey information in a fast, simple and effective way.

Understanding the text   **(Page 73)**

Question 1. Do you think Umberto Eco likes being interviewed? Give reasons for your opinion.

Answer Umberto Eco, the interviewee gives long and elaborate answers to the questions posed by Mukund Padmanabhan. He answers all the questions in a straightforward, truthful and sincere way, sharing his experiences with the world at large. Nowhere does he try to evade a question. He also smiles and shrugs during the interview which shows his interest. At no point, during the interview, we realise that he is in a hurry to wind up the interview.

Question 2. How does Eco find the time to write so much?

Answer Umberto Eco values time, in fact, each and every second. He utilizes even the 'interstices' *i.e.,* the empty spaces or gap between any two pieces of work. Most of us ignore this time but Umberto Eco makes its productive use. Thus, he has found time to write staggering amount of works.

Question 3. What was distinctive about Eco's academic writing style?

Answer Most of the writers attempting academic writing, have a depersonalized, dull and drab writing style. However, Umberto Eco has adopted an informal, playful and personalized writing style. It has a narrative element to it. He tells us the story of his research with all trials and errors. His writing not only gives information to the reader but tries to interest him too.

Question 4. Did Umberto Eco consider himself a novelist first or an academic scholar?

Answer Umberto Eco has over forty works in non-fiction, but only about five novels. The fictional works make him reach a large audience. He participates in academic conferences but not meetings of fan clubs and writers. This Professor thoroughly identifies himself with the academic community. He writes novels only when he is not involved in any scholarly activity and on Sundays.

Question 5. What is the reason for the huge success of the novel, 'The Name of the Rose'?

Answer The reason behind the success of 'The Name of the Rose' cannot be gauged. Umberto Eco himself calls the phenomenal success of the novel a mystery. Probably the detective novel that delves into metaphysics, theology and medieval history was written at the most appropriate time.

8

Going Places

AR Barton

Introduction

The story "Going Places" explores the theme of adolescent fantasising and hero-worship through the means of Sophie, the central character of the story who is a young girl. She lives in a dream world of her own often building castles in the air.

The author AR Barton brings into focus the dreams and aspirations of the youth, their ideals along with their fleeing and shattered dreams. He also highlights the complexities of human relationships by showcasing the role of family members and friends who try their best to help you in times of need. They are the ones who believe you through and through.

The Story Retold

Sophie's world of make believe and reality

Coming home from school, Sophie tells her friend, Jansie of her dream to own a boutique after leaving school. Jansie tries to bring her back into the world of reality by telling her that it required a lot of money. Sophie is calm and tells Jansie that she would manage but Jansie expresses her doubts by telling her that it would take long time to save so much.

Sophie refuses to come out of her dream world and says she will become a manager to save enough. Jansie wants her to do a reality check and realise that she wouldn't get the position straight away. Sophie does not bother and again starts dreaming of her boutique which she thinks would be the best in the city. Jansie feels sad because she knows that both of them are required to work in the biscuit factory after they pass out.

Jansie wishes that Sophie should not be carried away in her impossible-to-be realised dreams. Rather she should be sensible and practical. Sophie does not get affected by Jansie's protestations and emphasises on her dream to become an actress or a fashion designer to earn money and buy a boutique.

Sophie's family and her lower middle class background

Sophie's father disapproves of her pipe dreams and wishes she would buy them a decent house to live in just in case she ever runs into money. Derek, Sophie's younger brother retorts saying money doesn't grow on trees. Sophie's mother sighs at her daughter's dreams. Sophie's father works as hard as a manual labourer. Her mother's back has become crooked with the burden of household work. Her small house was suffocating and choking with steam from the stove and washing piled up in the corner.

Sophie's brother Geoff

Sophie shares an intimate relationship with him. He has been out of school for three years now. An apprentice mechanic, he is an enigmatic character. He is a man of few words and Sophie "suspected areas of his life about which she knew nothing". Sophie is jealous of his silence. She feels that he lives in the world of his own making. This world had a special fascination for her because it was not known to her and she could never visit it.

Sophie's impatience to visit the world unknown to her

Sophie expresses her longing to meet interesting, exotic people who she thinks are a part of her brother's world. She wants to be admitted more deeply into her brother's world. Her father forbids it because he thinks she is too young. Sophie is impatient to enter this vast world. She feels he will be at home in this romantic world. She imagines herself to be riding into this world with Geoff. She dreams that the whole world is waiting to receive her there.

Sophie reveals her dreams to Geoff

Sophie tells her brother Geoff about her meeting with Danny Casey in the arcade. Geoff refuses to believe her. Sophie says she met him when she was window shopping at the Royce's. She makes up details about his physical appearance for the story to sound authentic. Geoff shares her story with their father. Both dismiss her story as unrealistic and discuss the abilities of Danny Casey as a player. Their father warns Sophie that one day she will land herself in trouble because of her wild stories.

Sophie tries to make her story sound true

Sophie gives vivid details to Geoff about her meeting with Casey. She describes it as a chance encounter. She spoke first and also asked Casey for an autograph but could not since none of them had a paper or a pen. The two discussed about the clothes at Royce's. During the course of their conversation she felt that he was lonely, away from his home. They decide to meet next week and Casey promises to give her autograph then. Geoff still does not believe Sophie's story and says it is the 'unlikeliest' thing to happen.

The family goes to watch the match

Sophie, her father and Derek sit down near the goal while Geoff sits higher with his friends to watch the match. Danny Casey plays exceptionally well. He exhibits true Irish genius when he scores the second goal for United. He guides his team to two-nil victory. Sophie's father, brother Geoff and Derek express their happiness and celebrate the victory.

Sophie is shocked to find that Jansie knows of her meeting with Danny. Sophie tries to evade her questioning but fails. She admits to Jansie that she met the celebrity. Jansie knows Sophie's always in her dream world, cooking up things and refuses to believe her. Sophie realises that Jansie does not know anything about the date between her and Danny. Sophie is happy because Geoff had kept her faith in him. She tries to clear the mess by saying that it was all incidental. She explains to Jansie that she asked for Danny Casey's autograph but couldn't get it as there was no paper or pen. Jansie assures her that she can be trusted and leaves.

Sophie lives her dream

Sophie waits for Danny Casey at her favourite spot along the canal which was away from the hustle and bustle of the city. She considers it as the perfect place for a date.

She imagines Casey coming along the river and her own excitement thereafter. She tries hard to strike a balance between her dream world and the reality. She tries to balance the prospects of his coming with the prospects of his not coming. Her thoughts make her feel sad.

Sophie's dream now in shambles

Sophie's thinks how she will face her family members especially when no one believes what she had said. She is not ready to accept the reality and does not want to carry the burden of her sadness. She tries to imagine Geoff's disappointment when she tells him that Danny did not come. Though she feels sad and miserable but she does not want to give up her dream.

Sophie yet again transcends into the world of her make-believe

Sophie once again dreams of meeting Casey at Royce. In this meeting she tells Casey about his popularity with her family. She imagines asking him for the autograph once again. She feels his presence, his affinity to her in her imagination and is mesmerized to think that he is also a human being although a prodigy and a genius . She fails to come out of her fantasy and is overwhelmed by the memories of the match. This was the only time she had actually seen Danny Casey, her hero, in actuality.

Exercises

Think as you read (Page 79)

Question 1. Where was it most likely that the two girls would find work after school?

Answer The two girls were to be out of school just after a few months. They had no professional qualification nor financial resources to set up their own business. Belonging to lower middle class families, their parents had earmarked them for the biscuit factory. So, it was likely that they would find work in a biscuit factory after school.

Question 2. What were the options that Sophie was dreaming of? Why does Jansie discourage her from having such dreams?

Answer Sophie wanted to the break free from the barriers of her lower middle class background. She wished to buy a boutique if she has loads of money. She thinks she could be a manager somewhere and save money. Sophie even dreams of becoming an actress or a fashion designer. Earmarked for a biscuit factory, it was preposterous for her to live in such a dream world because it may have led to depression or low self-esteem.

Think as you read   (Page 81)

Question 1. Why did Sophie wriggle when Geoff told her father that she had met Danny Casey?

Answer   When Geoff told father about Sophie's chance encounter with Danny Casey, Sophie wriggled because she knew it was false. Her father was a practical, realistic person and Sophie was sure that he would reprimand her for concocting stories. She feared that she would have to add more details to the story to make it sound authentic.

Question 2. Does Geoff believe what Sophie says about her meeting with Danny Casey?

Answer   Geoff does not completely believe Sophie's story about her meeting with Danny Casey, the Irish football star. Although he had a strong bond with his sister as she shared all her secrets with him, he dismissed the whole story as the most unlikeliest thing. He does not hesitate to tell her that Casey would never keep his promise of meeting her again to give her the autograph.

Question 3. Does Sophie's father believe her story?

Answer   Sophie's father is a realist to the core. He does not believe in Sophie's story at all and dismisses it as another of her wild stories. When Geoff tells him about Sophie's chance encounter with Danny Casey, the Irish prodigy, he is not curious about it.

He changes the topic by saying that he once knew a man who knew Tom Finney. He warns Sophie that such concocted stories would land her into trouble some day.

Question 4. How does Sophie include her brother Geoff in her fantasy of her future?

Answer   Geoff has been out of school for three years and is working away from home as a mechanic. To Sophie, he is symbolic of freedom which she longs for. The unknown places he visited, the exotic, interesting people he met fascinated Sophie. She wished, he would take her into his fold. She knew a new world awaited them. She visualised herself riding behind Geoff. He wore black leathers and she wore yellow dress. With applause and aplomb the world rose to greet them.

Question 5. Which country did Danny Casey play for?

Answer   Danny Casey was a soccer player from Ireland. He was popular because he played really well. His technique was a blend of innocence and Irish genius. He drove his fans ecstatic when he struck the football into the goal. They were so overwhelmed with his genius that they wished he was an Englishman.

Think as you read   (Page 85)

Question 1. Why didn't Sophie want Jansie to know about her story with Danny?

Answer   Sophie did not want Jansie to know about her encounter with Danny Casey because Jansie was an expert at spreading rumours. Telling Jansie anything would be like telling the whole town. She feared that her father would get angry if her story of promixity with Casey spread in the town. Moreover, she had made up the story for Geoff only. She did not want people queuing up outside her house to enquire about the meeting.

Question 2. Did Sophie really meet Danny Casey?

Answer   No, Sophie did not meet Danny Casey in actuality at Royce's. Her story is a figment of her fantasy and imagination. She envisions her meeting with the Irish prodigy and concocts the minutest details which give the impression that she really met him.

Question 3. Which was the only occasion when she got to see Danny Casey in person?

Answer   The only occasion when Sophie got to see Danny Casey was when she went to watch the match with her family. Sitting amongst spectators, Sophie saw Casey from a distance. The power of her mind and fantasy was such that she concocted a story of her brief encounter with him and almost got an autograph from him!

Understanding the text   (Page 85)

Question 1. Sophie and Jansie were classmates and friends. What were the differences between them that show up in the story?

Answer   Although Sophie and Jansie were classmates and intimate friends, both of them had an altogether different approach towards life.

Jansie's feet are grounded in reality and she tries her best to pinpoint the reality. In contrast, Sophie is a dreamer who travels on the wings of imagination. Never for once in the story does she think practically or comes out of her dreamy world. Sophie harbours big and impossible dreams. Impossible because throughout the story we never see her making any efforts to realise them.

Jansie, on the other hand, knows that they have been earmarked for working in the biscuit factory and accepts her fate. Sophie seems immature and fickle-minded. In a single conversation, she wants to own a boutique, become a manager, an actress and even a fashion designer!

Jansie is a gossip monger who pokes her nose into other affairs. This is the reason why Sophie does not tell her about her meeting with Casey.

Sophie is a loving sister who admires her brother Geoff. She dreams of an exotic world that is waiting to take her into its fold. Sophie lives in a make-believe world where she befriends sports stars like Casey and is loved and admired by all. Jansie resigns to her fate and although of the same age does not indulge in fantasising and hero worship like Sophie.

Question 2. How would you describe the character and temperament of Sophie's father?

Answer Sophie's father is an archetypal man belonging to the lower working class. He is the sole provider of the family. We first meet him as a coarse, ill mannered man stuffing shepherd pie into his mouth, wearing his dirty and sweaty vest. Self-centred and exacting, he stops Sophie's wishful thinking by coercing her to think of buying them a decent house to move into just in case she makes big money.

He does not approve of Sophie's concocted story about meeting the Irish prodigy Danny Casey. He is a practical person who never leaves the world of harsh realities. He wants Sophie to step out of her dream world and start thinking worldy-wise. He tells her in a matter-of-fact tone, that her habit of making up stories is going to land her into trouble some day.

Although the family's financial condition is poor, it does not stop him and his family from going to watch the weekly football matches. He goes to the pub to celebrate something as frivolous as a football match. Thus, he is quite selfish.

Inspite of being the head of an impoverished family with so many mouths to feed, we never see him indulging in self-pity or cursing his fate. He rather enjoys his life to the fullest by making a weekly pilgrimage to watch United.

Question 3. Why did Sophie like her brother Geoff more than any other person? From her perspective, what did he symbolise?

Answer To Sophie, her brother Geoff symbolised liberty from her dull, drab, monotonous and impoverished existence. He had left school three years ago and was working away from home as an apprentice mechanic. He travelled everyday to work to the far side of the city and she imagined that he met many exotic and interesting people. They attained a special fascination for her, simply because they were unknown to her and remained out of her reach.

She wished in her heart of hearts that she could be admitted more deeply into her brother's affections and that someday he might take her with him. Sophie strongly felt that a whole new world was waiting for them and welcoming them into its fold. She felt that she was made for that world. She even imagined herself and Geoff to be a part of that glamorous world. Geoff was wearing new, shining black leathers and a yellow dress. "There was the sound of applause and the world rose to greet them".

Sophie liked Geoff because he was a man of few words. He patiently listened to her stories about meeting the sports icon Danny Casey although he suspects it is not true. He says it is the "unlikeliest" thing. Still he gives her the impression that he believed her. This made Sophie adore him more than she did any other member of her family.

Question 4. What socio-economic background did Sophie belong to? What are the indicators of her family's financial status?

Answer   Sophie belonged to the lower middle strata of the society. She had a working class background. She was to join a biscuit factory at meagre wages after completing her school. Her dreams of owing a boutique, becoming an actress or a fashion designer meant nothing for her family.

Sophie's father was an archetypal working man perhaps doing manual labour to make both ends meet. A coarse and ill-mannered man, he lacked the sense and refinement to appreciate Sophie's aspirations to seek better prospects. Sophie's mother was so involved in household chores that her back had become bent. She sighs on hearing her daughter's dreams. She does not support her nor contradicts her husbands's views.

Derek, her little brother echoes her father's views when he says that Sophie thinks money grows on trees. Her father wants that just in case she lands herself into big money, she should buy a decent house for the family to live in. Sophie is repelled at the sight of her father in a stinky vest, his face grimy and sweaty. The small room steamy from the stove and cluttered with dirty washing piled up in the corner, detest her.

All these indicate that Sophie does not belong to a very well-off family.

Talking about the text   (Page 85-86)

Question 5. Sophie's dreams and disappointments are all in her mind.

Answer   Sophie lived in her own world of dreams. She wanted to materialize those things which were simply not possible on practical grounds. Like her father she was also a great fan of football and Danny Casey. She sees him only once in action scoring the second goal for United. After that she was always lost in the thoughts of Daney Casey. She imagined him coming and talking to her. She waited for him for a long time. She knew he wouldn't come and became sad and disappointed. She imagined so several times which reveals that she was an incurable dreamer and escapist.

Thus, it would not be wrong to say that all dreams and disappointments were in her mind. They were the products of her fantasy and imagination.

Question 6. It is natural for teenagers to have unrealistic dreams. What would you say are the benefits and disadvantages of such fantasising? Explain this statement in the light of the chapter, "Going Places".

Answer   Dreaming is a necessary part of one's life. Without dreams, there will be no aims and aspirations in our lives. We will have nothing to look forward to or struggle our way to the top.

Teenage is a natural process through which every human being goes through. At this age, everybody indulges in hero worship and fantasising. This is what happens with Sophie also. She idolises Danny Casey to the extent that she is involved in a romantic liason with him! If only she had dreamt of him for becoming a soccer player, this would have changed her fortune forever. We cannot solely put the blame on her for this. Her dreams are unrealistic and she views the world with rose-coloured glasses.

Her longing for earning big bucks forces her to dream of opening a boutique, become an actress or a fashion designer. Undoubtedly, it is important to dream high. If one doesn't one cannot achieve anything in life. However, unrealistic dreams which are not within our reach can be damaging to our personality, unrealistic goals which are beyond our capacity can lead to depression, low self-esteem and suicidal tendencies.

Thus, dreams are a part and parcel of our lives. We cannot do without them but we must remember that if we go overboard with them, they might have a negative effect on our personalities. We should not end up like Sophie, who carried the burden of her shattered dreams in despair.

1

My Mother at Sixty-Six

Kamala Das

Introduction

'The poem has been written in lyrical idom and it brings out the complex subtleties of human relationships. The poetess who had gone to meet her mother is returning. Her mother accompanies her to the airport. On the way, her mother dozes off. The poetess is very upset seeing her mother's pale face which is withering day by day. The significant thing about the poem is that the whole poem is in a single sentence, punctuated by commas. This indicates a single line of thought peppered with occasional observations of the real world.

Stanzawise Explanation of the Poem

1. *Driving from my .... of their homes.*

The poetess had gone to her home-town to visit her mother. On Friday morning, she was returning. She was driving down to the airport at Cochin. Her mother had accompanied her to the airport to see her off. On the way, when the poet turned to her old mother, she saw that her old mother had dozed off and her mouth was slightly open. Her face was pale and lifeless just like a dead person's face. The poetess is pained to see her mother's face which is an image of aging and decay.

The poetess is very disturbed and alarmed to see the condition of her mother. To change her thoughts, she looks the other way. She sees lush green trees which are speeding away in the opposite direction. This is so because the car was moving at a great speed. This is a grim reminder of the fact that time has passed at a fast pace. She also sees a group of children who are coming out of their home in a jiffy. They represent the exuberance and vigour of youth. Perhaps, they also make her nostalgic as they remind her of the time when her mother was young. Their youth is a contrast to her mother's senility and declining years.

2. *But after the .... smile and smile.*
After reaching the airport and going through the security check, the poetess who was standing a few yards away from her mother, once again looks at her mother's lifeless, deteriorating, faded face which seems dull and colourless like a late winter's moon. Once again, she is pained, on seeing her mother's deteriorating condition and is torn apart by a fear whether she would see her mother alive next time. She puts away such desponding thoughts and very optimistically bids her mother good bye, "Amma see you soon". She smiles reassuringly at her mother and keeps smiling at her cheerfully.

Literary Devices Used in the Poem

   I. Simile

       her face ashen like that of a corpse

       wan, pale as a late winter's moon

  II. Repetition

       thought away .... thought away

       smile and smile and smile

  III. Symbols and Imagery

       young trees sprinting, merry children spilling,

       winter's moon

Exercises

Before you read   (Page 90)

Ageing is a natural process; have you ever thought what our elderly parents expect from us?

Answer Aged people usually undergo pangs of loneliness and need companionship. They long only for our love, care and attention. They expect their children to share the happenings in their lives with them and take their suggestions for making significant decisions. This will encourage them to live life enthusiastically.

Think it out (Page 91)

Question 1. What is the kind of pain and ache that the poet feels?

Answer The poet is pained to see her mother's pale ashen face which almost looks like that of a corpse. The poet gets nostalgic as she reminisces the time when her mother was youthful. She is torn apart by the fear of not seeing her mother alive next time. She visits her hometown. The growing pain, insecurity and fear of her childhood that she would lose her mother comes back again and again.

Question 2. Why are the young trees described as 'sprinting'?

Answer The poet describes the young trees as sprinting, as the car is moving at a great speed and the trees on the road side are being passed at a fast space which makes them seem as if they are running along. This also contrasts with the poet's "ashen like" old mother who has weakened with time. Secondly, it also points out to the disparity that the trees are 'sprinting' whereas the mother is dozing.

Question 3. Why has the poet brought in the image of the merry children 'spilling out of their homes'?

Answer The poet has used this effect to bring out the contrast between children who are energetic, exuberant and enthusiastic. In contrast to them, the mother is old, pale and asleep. She is an image of ageing decay whereas the children epitomise bubbly youth. Perhaps, the poet is reminded of the days when her mother too represented the same spirit like the children.

Question 4. Why has the mother been compared to the 'late winter's moon'?

Answer The poet has used a simile as 'the late winter's moon' looks too hazy and lacks brightness and lustre. Similarly, the mother who is now sixty six is pale and has a shrunken and ashen face which is like a corpse. She is devoid of the effervescence and exhilaration of youth. The comparison is very apt to bring out the required effect.

Question 5. What do the parting words of the poet and her smile signify?

Answer The poet's parting words and her smile are a facade to hide her feelings of insecurity. The pale and senile appearance of her mother, brings her focus into childhood fear of losing her mother. She can definitely experience the pangs of separation yet she bids her farewell in a pleasant manner. She reassures her mother that all will be well till the time they meet again.

2

An Elementary School Classroom in a Slum

Stephen Spender

Introduction

Stephen Spender was an English poet and an essayist. He took a keen interest in politics and declared himself to be a socialist and pacifist. In, 'An Elementary School Classroom in a Slum', he has brought out the pathetic condition of the slum children. He vehemently opposes the social injustice which denies the very basic right to education to children. He decries the class inequalities and government apathy in this poem.

Stanzawise Explanation of the Poem

1. *Far far from .... other than this.*

The poet vividly portrays the pathetic conditions of children in a slum school. The children studying in a class of slum area are far away from a world abounding in nature's bounties and lighter aspects of life. Their world is instead full of squalor and harsh realities. These children have a pathetic look. They have pale faces and their hair is unkempt, falling all over their faces, making them look like rootless weeds.

In the classroom, there is a tall girl who has put her head down. She is very depressed, may be due to abject poverty or family tussles. The boy who is sitting in the corner is reed thin, almost like paper, he has big bulging eyes like that of a rat. This metaphor suggests his timid nature and search for food and security. Yet another boy is the heir of his father's gnarled disease. He has a stunted growth and is sitting there at his desk with his twisted bones. He is a living example of his father's 'knotty' disease.

There is no enthusiasm in him. Another character is a sweet natured boy who is sitting at the back of that dingy classroom. He is not a prominent character. He is sitting there and dreaming of squirrel games. He would have preferred to be out of this classroom in the open.

2. *On sour cream .... stars of words.*

The dull and monotonous routine fails to attract him. The walls of this dingy classroom are dirty yellow. Painted long ago, they don't seem to motivate and engross the students. In the corner, Shakespeare's portrait has been stuck. This is ironic because the children are so caught up in the rut of life that all this is meaningless. Early in the morning, the sky is clear and cloudless. The domes of institutions glimmer in every city. But these pictures have no significance for these children who have not seen anything except the dingy slums.

There is also a picture of a beautiful valley adorned with fragrant flowers. However, the children can never ever experience this fascinating sight as they are condemned to live a life devoid of all joys and jubilation. The map in the classroom should offer limitless opportunities to students. It should act like their window to the world. But unfortunately it is not so.

Their world outside is grim, uncertain and full of trials and tribulations. The poet conveys a dismal view of their world by using the metaphor of fog. Just as fog in the winters blurs one's view, the slum children's future is blurred with hopelessness, indignity and hunger. Their future is in the shackles of narrow, dusty streets and sealed with a dark and dull sky. These children are far away from the dreamy world of gurgling rivers, snow-covered mountains and luminous stars.

3. *Surely, Shakespeare is .... big as doom.*

Shakespeare doesn't mean anything to these children nor does the map on the wall which shows them the world for their world is merely their classroom. Rather the beautiful world with all its allurements such as the warm sun, beautiful ships only tempt the children to run away from their miserable surroundings and cramped lives. Their houses are small almost like narrow holes. There is no end to their miserable life which begins with fog and ends with the same. The poet is appalled at the fact that there is no redeemer here. They live in these dreary places from birth to death. They spend their childhood in garbage heaps.

Some of the children living in these areas are very skinny and have their bones peeping out of their skins. They use steel spectacles, the glasses of which are cracked and look like broken pieces of bottle on stone. It is their lot to use the discarded things of the rich. It seems they are living in a perpetual state of gloom and despair. These children are destined to spend all their life in these living hells. These slums are a blot on the civilized world, the world of the privileged. The worst thing is that these children are unable to locate their slums on the map.

4. *Unless, governor .... the sun.*

These deplorable conditions will continue for these children until governors, inspectors and visitors take keen interest to bridge this chasm. The map hanging in their classroom becomes their window to the world because it is only through it that they can see the world which is so different from their slums. The windows of their classroom just confine them to their melancholic world. It seems that the lives of these children of a lesser God are sealed in the cemetries of filthy slums.

The poet fervently appeals to the educated and the bourgeoisie, the capitalists or 'haves' in Marxist ideology to alleviate the miseries of the children belonging to slums. He earnestly wants that the children should be free to stroll in the green fields and run on the golden sands without any worldly worries. Childhood should be innocent and carefree. The poet desires it to be so for the children of the slums. They should have access to education. They should be allowed to read books and be given countless opportunities to explore the world. They need to break free from the confines of their bleak world into a world which should welcome them with open arms. The poet exhorts that the unfeeling, self-centred attitude of the affluent classes ought to be broken to relieve the children of all misery.

Literary Devices Used in the Poem

I. Simile	**III. Use of Imagery and Symbols**
like rootless weeds	rootless weeds
like bottle bits on stones	Shakespeare's head
like catacombs	open handed map
slums as big as doom	bottle bits on stones
II. Metaphor	ships and sun
rat's eyes	cramped holes
father's gnarled disease	gold sands
squarrel's game	gusty waves
tree room	paper-seeming boy
future's painted with fog	sour cream walls
lead sky	Tyrolese valley
spectacles of steel	

Exercises

Before you read (Page 92)

Have you ever visited or seen an elementary school in a slum? What does it look like?

Answer Yes, I have visited such a school; it was a government school. It was in a pitiful state. It did not have even the basic amenities like properly working fans and lights or separate toilets for girls. Even drinking water was not available. Broken windows, damaged doors, broken benches and dirty walls greeted the students. Many of the teachers did not conduct the classes regularly.

Think it out (Page 92)

Question 1. Tick the item which best answers the following

    (a) The tall girl with her head weighed down means
       The girl
         (i) is ill and exhausted
         (ii) has her head bent with shame
         (iii) has untidy hair

    (b) The paper seeming boy with rat's eyes means
       The boy is
         (i) thin, hungry and weak
         (ii) sly and secretive
         (iii) unpleasant looking

    (c) The stunted unlucky heir of twisted bones means
       The boy
         (i) has an inherited disability
         (ii) was short and long

    (d) His eyes live in a dream. A squirrel's game, in the tree room other than this means
       The boy is
         (i) full of hope in the future
         (ii) mentally ill
         (iii) distracted from the lesson

  (e) The children's faces are compared to 'rootless weeds'
     This means they
     (i) are insecure
     (ii) are ill-fed
    (iii) are wasters

Answer   (a) (i) is ill and exhausted
          (b) (ii) thin, hungry and weak
          (c) (i) has an inherited disability
          (d) (iii) idstracted from the lesson
          (e) (ii) are ill-fed

Question 2. What do you think is the colour of 'sour cream'? Why do you think the poet has used this expression to describe the classroom walls?

Answer The colour of the sour cream is pale yellow. The poet has used this expression to show the poor and grim environment of the classroom. Instead of bringing cheer to the unhappy existence of the children, these walls add to their misery and dreariness.

Question 3. The walls of the classroom are decorated with the pictures of 'Shakespeare', 'buildings with domes', 'world maps' and 'beautiful valleys'. How do these contrast with the world of these children?

Answer 'Shakespeare' symbolises the study of literature, 'buildings with domes' stand for power and riches, the 'world maps' represent, the world outside and 'beautiful valleys' refer to the nature's beauty and bounty. All this stands in sharp contrast to the dingy, dismal and gloomy atmosphere in which these slum children live.

Question 4. What does the poet want for the children of the slums? How can their lives be made to change?

Answer The poet wants that the children of the slums should get rid of their dismal lives. They should have the right to education which will be the agent of change in their lives. The apathy of the affluent classes towards them has to come to an end. The children should be able to enjoy the intrinsic beauty of nature and break down all barriers that confine them to such gloomy life.

3

Keeping Quiet

Pablo Neruda

Introduction

Man is always in a jiffy with no time for himself. His own actions are the cause of many of his miseries. Pablo Neruda in this poem has emphasised on the importance of introspection and silence which can help man in solving many of his problems whose basis is caste, religion and nationality. The poet gives a clarion call for breaking the barriers of hatred and violence by remaining mute through the medium of meditation exercise.

Stanzawise Explanation of the Poem

1. *Now we will .... arms so much.*

The poet exhorts each one of us to count twelve and then be quiet, silent and motionless so that at least for once no language will be spoken on the surface of the earth. In this moment of tranquillity the poet doesn't want anyone to move their arms.

2. *It would be .... sudden strangeness.*

The poet feels that would be a very enticing moment because no one will be in a hurry. There would be no sound of machines to pollute the atmosphere. It will be a very strange moment with stillness all around with which we would be unfamiliar. But it would be an unusual period in which we would all be together in a condition which is foremost for the survival of humanity.

3. *Fishermen in the .... his hurt hands.*

In this moment of silence and inactivity, the fishermen would not be catching fish and the whale in the cold waters will be safe. Also, the man who gathers salt will be able to tend to his wounded hands which otherwise he had no time for.

4. *Those who prepare .... shade doing nothing.*

The poet observes that for once those who are waging wars be it against the environment or against other human beings by using poisonous gas or fire, must stop their destructive tasks. Instead, they should take this opportunity to wear clean clothes and walk with their brothers building mutual trust and brotherhood. In that split second, there will also be complete harmony between human beings and nature.

5. *What I want .... ourselves with death.*

The poet says while he is propagating silence, his advice should not be confused with total inactivity, that is death, for he doesn't want any association with death. What he is advising people is they should neither be self centred nor stoop or resort to dubious ways to meet their selfish ends. They should not just think of only keeping their lives moving. What he wants is that people should rest for a while.

For once they should not do anything. It will do them good for they will get time for introspection. They will be able to understand themselves and know what they want in life. This would help in overcoming their sadness of failing to understand themselves. Also, when we are only threatening ourselves with death, this moment of silence can really help us to understand ourselves.

6. *Perhaps the Earth .... I will go.*

The poet feels that the Earth enlightens us of the fact that how all life processes come to an end and then begin all over again. *e.g.,* in the winter season everything appears to be dormant and lifeless. In contrast to this spring is abuzz with activity and life. Talking in the similar vein, the poet feels that from this moment of tranquillity we can bring all evil and wicked thoughts to a standstill and begin a new life where there is no frenzied desire to work without break.

We should live in unison with each other and the forces of nature. With this perception in mind, the poet calls, for a deep introspection and contemplation in order to find a true spirit of brotherhood and understanding among fellow human beings.

Exercises

Before you read (Page 95)

What does the title of the poem suggest to you? What do you think the poem is about?

Answer The title of the poem suggests the importance of silence. The poem is about the importance of quiet introspection for all. Our speech and activities often bring about trouble and suffering, so they need to be controlled.

Think it out (Page 96)

Question 1. What will counting upto twelve and keeping still help us achieve?

Answer Twelve here represents the markings of a clock. The poet wants us to count upto twelve and then keep quiet. It will help us to understand ourselves and realise the frenzy which is keeping us pre-occupied with materialism. In a moment of tranquillity, the poet fervently hopes that we may find answers to our problems.

Question 2. Do you think the poet advocates total inactivity and death?

Answer No, the poet clearly states that his asking for stillness should not be confused with inactivity. He perceives life to be a continuous process where man's activities should not lead to destruction of fellow human beings or nature but channelized in a resourceful way.

Question 3. What is the 'sadness' that the poet refers to in the poem?

Answer The poet refers to the sadness which surrounds man due to not having any time for himself, of not understanding what he or his fellow human beings want. He has no time for introspection, with a result he is unable to analyse his own actions and understand its consequences.

Question 4. What symbol from nature does the poet invoke to say that there can be life under apparent stillness?

Answer The poet associates death with total inactivity and stillness. By giving a clarion call for keeping silence, the poet wants us to understand that the cycle of life along with its life processes goes on. Nature carries on its work even when there is stillness all around. For example, winter is associated with inactivity but it is not really true. Spring, on the other hand, is synonymous with liveliness.

4

A Thing of Beauty

John Keats

Introduction

John Keats was a British romantic poet who decided to devote himself wholly to poetry. The following is an excerpt from his poem *'Endymion A Poetic Romance'*. The poem is based on a Greek legend, in which Endymion, a beautiful young shepherd and a poet who lived on Mount Latmos had a vision of Cynthia, the moon goddess. The enchanted youth resolved to seek her out and so wandered away through the forest and down under the sea.

Stanzawise Explanation of the Poem

1. *"A thing .... quiet breathing."*

Through his wonderful gift of perceiving the world and living his moods and aspirations in terms of language, Keats expresses the fact that beautiful things give us eternal pleasure. A beautiful object gives us limitless joy. There is no time frame for the happiness it gives us. It is everlasting and leaves an indelible image in our minds. The sight of the beautiful object is stored in our memory like a cool and pleasant bower (here, bower refers to a pleasant place which is in the shade of trees). Another comparison which the poet gives us is in the form of sweet dreams which bring to our mind those lovely sights that give us tremendous joy. These memories may also come back when we are at peace with ourselves, quietly breathing or meditating. Thus, the poet echoes the feeling that beautiful things ought to be cherished and treasured.

2. *"Therefore, on every .... our dark spirits".*

The poet feels that every morning we prepare a wreath of flowers that strengthens our bond with the Earth. In other words, we make a string of flowers or memories which help us recall the bounties and the picturesque sights of the Earth. These act as a motivating tool which strengthens us.

Despondency and disappointment are a part and parcel of human life and we are often at a loss due to the self-centred and wicked nature of others. Still there comes a glimmer of hope when a wonderful sight or object gives us pleasure. We are, thus, able to shun sad and gloomy thoughts away, giving way to hope and optimism.

3. *"Such the Sun, ...musk-rose blooms".*

As a poet Keats feels that one can find beauty even in the simplest things, like the Sun and the Moon. The various objects of nature abound in beauty. He appreciates the scenic and serene beauty of nature through trees, the sheep, the daffodils and even the green pastures and streams. The trees provide us protection through the means of shade. Sheep are a symbol of divine beauty whereas the lush green surroundings are an embodiment of joy and delight. The streams have an exalting effect on human beings. Their graphic view has a cooling effect as compared to the scorching heat of the summers.

Another vivid view that gives us immense pleasure is when suddenly we come across wild roses growing amidst a forest.

4. *"And such too .... heaven's brink".*

Keats feels that there is beauty not only in growth but also decay. Similarly, birth is followed by death. Both are inseparable and there is beauty in both these aspects.

Beauty and joy is also inherent in the fall or death of mighty emperors who made innumerable sacrifices. It becomes a source of motivation for all those who read or hear these valourous tales. Thus, beauty is referred to an 'endless fountain' *i.e.*, an eternal source of motivation, an elixir of life, a precious gift from heaven which gives us infinite pleasure and delight.

Exercises

Before you read   (Page 98)

What pleasure does a beautiful thing give us? Are beautiful things worth treasuring?

Answer A beautiful thing gives us everlasting joy and pleasure. Beautiful things are worth treasuring because their memory soothes our nerves and inspires us to overcome the depressing elements in life.

Think it out   (Page 99)

Question 1. List the things of beauty mentioned in the poem.

Answer Some of the things mentioned in the poem are the Sun, the Moon, young and old trees, flowers like daffodils, streams with clear water, ferns and musk-roses. All these according to the poet are a perennial source of joy.

Question 2. List the things that cause suffering and pain.

Answer Life is full of suffering and pain. Some of the things which are the cause of sufferings are malice, disappointments, lack of noble qualities, unhealthy and evil ways of life which become the cause of much unhappiness. They dampen our spirit and bring sadness to one's life.

Question 3. What does the line, 'Therefore are we wreathing a flowery band to bind us to earth' suggest to you?

Answer Things of beauty are those 'bands' which keep us tied to the earth inspite of all its sorrows. Every morning we revive our memories which consist of beautiful sights and objects, so that we may be motivated to continue our journey of life which may otherwise be painful.

Question 4. What makes human beings love life inspite of troubles and sufferings?

Answer Things of beauty conceal all our sadness and cause of suffering. They bring us happiness and love and motivate us to continue our journey of life inspite of all our troubles and sufferings.

Question 5. Why is 'grandeur' associated with the 'mighty dead'?

Answer Beauty for Keats should not only be aesthetically pleasing, but it should be intellectual and spiritual as well. The death of a mighty emperor is replete with intellectual and spiritual beauty. Birth, growth and decay, both are inseparable. Each has its own beauty. Death is beautiful because it makes us immortal.

Question 6. Do we experience things of beauty only for short moments or do they make a lasting impression on us?

Answer Being a Romantic, Keats believed, "A thing of beauty is a joy forever." They are a constant source of joy and inspiration and leave a lasting impression on us. There is no time frame for the happiness it gives us.

Question 7. What image does the poet use to describe the beautiful bounty of the earth?

Answer The poet uses the image of an 'endless fountain' which showers bounties on earth. He calls this 'immortal drink' from the heavens. The sun, the moon, the trees, the sheep, the daffodils, the lushgreen forests and streams reflect the beautiful bounties which God has given us.

5

A Roadside Stand

Robert Frost

Introduction

Robert Frost is a highly acclaimed American poet of the twentieth century. He wrote about characters, people and landscapes. In the poem, Frost presents the pathetic conditions of the poor deprived people. He has done this with pitiless clarity and with deep sympathy and humanity. Everyone pretends to be their benefactor but are actually 'greedy good-doers'.

Stanzawise Explanation of the Poem

1. *The little old house .... and go along.*

On the roadside there is an old house which has an extended shed. This shed is towards the edge of the road. The owners have made this towards the edge so that the fast moving vehicles speeding by may notice and stop there to buy the food and refreshments sold there.

This shed made a pitiable site, it almost seemed as if it was begging for food but that was not so. Rather it was made so that the rich people who passed by the shed in their beautiful cars would stop there and buy something, so that some cash would flow into the hands of the owners, who then would be able to buy some of the things that are sold in the city.

The poor feel that the money the rich spend to adorn their gardens with flowers can be used to better the lot of the less privileged. But, the rich people passed by without paying any attention to the shed. If anyone cared to stop, it was only due to the irritation at the paint and decor of poor taste that was marring the picturesque scenery of the area. Also, the shed had a board on which the directions were written but they were pointing incorrectly; for the north was pointing towards the South and *vice-versa*. This shed sold wild berries in wooden boxes. Also, they sold squash which was in bottles which had crooked necks and silver lids.

Besides these things, the place also offered a stay in the scenic surroundings. However, the travellers felt that these poorly kept stands spoiled the pristine beauty of the landscape. The rich who passed by the place had the money but had no desire to spend it. According to the people they were mean and miserly. They wanted to keep the money with themselves.

2. *The hurt to the scenery .... keeping from us.*

The poet does not want to accuse the rustics of marring the beauty of the landscape. He is more worried about the untold pain that unsaid words cause to the faith of the people belonging to the countryside. The rustics have set-up a roadside stand so far away in these inhospitable mountains just to earn some hard cash. They long to have a comfortable lifestyle as depicted in movies. They hope against hope that the city denizens may fulfil the promise of giving them economic independence although it was in the purview of the party in power to do so.

3. *It is in the .... the ancient way.*

It is in news that these countryside folks are to be relocated in the villages where they will have all comforts. They will enjoy privileges of the theatre and store just like their urban counterparts. So busy will be these people in enjoying these comforts that they will have no time to think about themselves or fight for their rights. The 'haves' are called 'beasts of prey' because in the garb of benefits that they will provide to the rustics, they will exploit them to no end. Later the privileged ones will easily forget their promises leaving these poor people more impoverished.

4. *Sometimes I feel .... didn't it see?*

The poet is very disturbed and feels very helpless when he sees their childish longing for money which is never fulfilled. These people keep their windows open all day as if in prayer waiting desperately and uselessly for someone to stop at the stand. Sadness at their disappointment can be noticed all around the place when no one stops there. Out of thousands of cars passing by, just one stopped only to inquire the prices of things sold there. Another stopped just to use the backyard of the place to reverse their car. Yet another stopped just to inquire where the road led to. The fourth stopped to knew if they could sell them a gallon of gas (petrol). The farmer grumbles in an angry manner that couldn't they see for themselves that it was not sold there. Actually, the country people are upset over the callous attitude of city dwellers. Moreover, it shows the chasm between the thinking of the city denizens and the stark reality of the rural people.

5. *No, in country .... of my pain.*

Finally the poet bemoans that the spirit to scale new heights to break the shackles of economic dependency is not present in the rustics. That is why they do not stop complaining against the economic inequalities. The poet strongly feels that the countryside people should be freed from the pain of poverty and deprivation. Next morning when the poet gains his senses, he wonders what if someone else thinks in the same manner for him so that he is gently relieved from his pain and agony of seeing the miserable condition of these people.

Exercises

Before you read   (Page 100)

Have you ever stopped at a roadside stand? What have you observed there?

Answer Yes, I have stopped at such places while motoring on highways. They are owned by poor people who live in the countryside near to the highway. Generally they sell local produce such as foodstuffs, fruits or items of daily use. The quality varies from stand to stand and you can bargain for reducing the quoted price if you want to really buy something from them.

Think it out   (Page 102)

Question 1. The city folk who drove through the countryside hardly paid any heed to the roadside stand or to the people who ran it. If at all they did, it was to complain. Which lines bring this out? What was their complaint about?

Answer The following lines bring out the complaining attitude of the city people who drove by the shed in the countryside.

'.............. then out of sorts'
At having the landscape marred with the artless paint.

'Of signs that with N turned wrong and S turned wrong'. The complaint of these passers-by was that the artless paint was spoiling the pristine beauty of the landscape. They were displeased that the board out there had signs of N and S pointing to the wrong directions. Moreover, they were critical of wild berries being sold in wooden quarts.

Question 2. What was the plea of the folk who had put up the roadside stand?

Answer   The folks who had put up the roadside stand wanted the passers-by to stop and buy the berries or the squash which they sold so that they could have some ready cash which they could improve their lot and better their miserable lives.

Question 3. The government and other social service agencies appear to help the poor rural people, but actually do them no good. Pick out the words and phrases that the poet uses to show their double standards.

Answer   The government and the party which is in power were least interested in the welfare of these poor rural people. Even the social service agencies were doing nothing for them. They have their own vested interests. The words and phrases which show their double standards are

'greedy good doers', 'beneficent beasts of prey', 'swam over their lives', 'enforcing benefits', 'calculated', 'to soothe them out of their wits.'

Question 4. What is the 'childish longing' that the poet refers to? Why is it 'vain'?

Answer   'Childish longing' literally means to want and wait for something without putting logic in it. The longing is in a way innocent also. Similarly, the poet refers the longing of the people running the roadside stand as childish because they are always waiting for prospective customers. They keep their windows open to attract customers and become sad when nobody turns up. They hope that some car will stop there but their waiting goes in 'vain' when they see that people come either to turn their cars or to ask where the way goes.

Question 5. Which lines tell us about the insufferable pain that the poet feels at the thought of the plight of the rural poor?

Answer   The poet intensely feels that all the miserable pains from which the poor rustics suffer from must be removed at one stroke. The following lines express his feelings.

'I can't help owning the great relief it would be,
To put these people at one stroke out of their pain'.

6

Aunt Jennifer's Tigers

Adrienne Rich

Introduction

The poet, Adrienne Rich was born in Baltimore, Maryland (USA). She is well known for her active involvement in the feminist movement. Her work reflects a strong opposition to racism and militarism. The poem 'Aunt Jennifer's Tigers' addresses the issues of gender conflict, oppression of women, male dominance and restraint of custom and law on women in a sutle tone. Aunt Jennifer is a timid woman who makes a make-believe world of her own. She is bogged down by the shackles of male chauvinism as personified by her tyrant husband.

Stanzawise Explanation of the Poem

1. *Aunt Jennifer's .... chivalric certainty.*

Steeped in feminism, the poet potrays a vivid criticism of a male dominated societal set-up. Aunt Jennifer has been reduced to a quivering woman who is terrified. She weaves a world of her own where there are tigers leaping and prancing about. The tigers belong to the jungle and stand in contrast to Aunt Jennifer — they are fearless. They symbolise the free spirit of liberation which Aunt Jennifer yearns for. The first few lines bring out the patriarchial attitude and discrimination against women.

2. *Aunt Jennifer's .... Jennifer's hand.*

Aunt Jennifer is so terrorized that her fingers are unable to carry the weight of even something as light as wool! She is a victim who has been so oppressed that she is unable to pull the ivory needle. The uncle's wedding ring seems to be heavy to her because it weighed her down by the burden of marital responsibilities and subjugated her completely. Societal conventions are also to be blamed for reducing her to a tyrannized woman. She fears her husband so much that even in his absence she is not comfortable.

3. *When Aunt .... and unafraid.*

The poet says that even death will not be able to release Aunt Jennifer from the trials and tribulations which she had to undergo in her lifetime. The trauma she had to face will linger on. However, the embroidery she has done will survive for eternity. The tigers she has knitted will remain fearless as ever continuing their search for a prey. In other words, the tigers which symbolise male dominance and suppression continue their horrifying victimization. No societal set-up or custom can stop men from torturing and terrorizing the weaker sex. The metaphor of tiger very aptly describes the intentions of a male dominated set-up.

Another meaning which can be gauged from the last few lines is that perhaps, the prancing tigers represent Aunt Jennifer's intense longing for freedom and desire to live life on her own terms.

Symbols and Images Used In the Poem

The tiger has been used as a symbol of male domination, oppression and fear which Aunt Jennifer and countless women like her have to undergo. It is also symbolic of her desire and craving for freedom which she is not able to achieve even after death.

The Uncle's wedding band is symbolic of constraints imposed upon Aunt Jennifer by matrimony, customs and law. It represents the domineering male.

The fluttering wool is an image which shows how cowed down is Aunt Jennifer due to ordeals of her conjugal life. She has been victimized so much that her hands cannot bear the burden of something as light as wool. Her husband has overshadowed her so completely that she does not have any individuality of her own.

Ringed with ordeals is an image which expresses the fact that Aunt Jennifer's life is a saga of oppression, gender bias and constraints. She is a silent sufferer who does not raise her voice even after death.

Exercises

Before you read   (Page 103)

What does the title of the poem suggest to you? Are you reminded of other poems on tigers?

Answer   The title of the poem suggests that it is about Aunt Jennifer's knitted tigers which become an alternate world created by her to free herself from the burden of married life. She is expressing her fear and struggle in married life and her desire to be free through her knitting. 'The Tiger' by William Blake and 'Tiger' by Alec D Hope are some other famous poems on tigers.

Think it out   (Page 104)

Question 1. How do 'denizens' and 'chivalric' add to our understanding of the tiger's attitudes?

Answer   'Denizens' means occupants and 'Chivalric' refers to fearlessness and majesty. Tigers are very possessive about their domain. They live on their own terms and fear none. The poet finds similarities between the disposition of tigers and men.

Question 2. Why do you think Aunt Jennifer's hands are 'fluttering through her wool' in the second stanza? Why is she finding the needle so hard to pull?

Answer   Aunt Jennifer has a troubled married life with a domineering and oppressive husband. She tries to find refuge in art, but even here, she cannot leave behind the weight of her conjugal life. Thus, her hands quiver so much that she cannot pull even the needles through the base cloth.

Question 3. What is suggested by the image 'massive weight of Uncle's wedding band'?

Answer   It suggests the difficulties which Aunt Jennifer has been through in her married life. The wedding is symbolic. It represents the unbreakable bond of love and commitment between the husband and wife but in Aunt Jennifer's case it refers to bondage, restrictions and overbearing nature of her husband.

Question 4. Of what or of whom is Aunt Jennifer terrified with in the third stanza?

Answer   Aunt Jennifer has passed through many testing times during her married life. These times have suppressed her. She was dominated by them not only during her lifetime but even after her death. The dominating, callous and cold attitude of her husband continues to haunt her even after death.

Question 5. What are the 'ordeals' Aunt Jennifer is surrounded by? Why is it significant that the poet uses the word 'ringed'? What are the meanings of the word 'ringed' in the poem?

Answer Aunt Jennifer is surrounded by the trials and tribulations of her conjugal life. The word 'ringed' refers to bondage. Aunt Jennifer is bound by the conventions of matrimony and the whims and wishes of her overbearing husband. She has sacrificed her personal liberty. Another connotation of the word can be a ring in the circus where Aunt Jennifer is the oppressed and the uncle an oppressor.

Question 6. Why do you think Aunt Jennifer created animals that are so different from her own character? What might the poet be suggesting through this difference?

Answer Aunt Jennifer is a weak and terrified person who was suppressed by the constraints of marriage all her life. The animals that she is creating in her panel are very different as they are chivalric and do not fear men. They are a symbol of strength, fierceness and beauty. The poet wants to emphasize on the spirit and desire for freedom which is innate in all human beings.

Question 7. Interpret the symbols found in this poem.

Answer The 'tiger' is symbolic of oppression and cruelty through which women like Aunt Jennifer have been victimized by men. They also represent the spirit of freedom for which Aunt Jennifer yearns for. 'Uncle's wedding band' symbolises male domination and constraints imposed by the society in the garb of marriage.

Question 8. Do you sympathise with Aunt Jennifer? What is the attitude of the speaker towards Aunt Jennifer?

Answer Yes, Aunt Jennifer deserves our sympathy. She is victimized by the unfeeling, domineering and cold attitude of her husband. Even the speaker is sympathetic towards her. In the last stanza of the poem, she expresses her feelings that even after death Aunt Jennifer continues to live in fear of her tyrannical husband.

1

The Third Level

Jack Finney

Introduction

The story deals with the curious experience of a 31 year old man, Charley, a daily commuter who reaches the 'third level' while taking the subway for his home.

In reality there are only two level of stations of New York's Grand Central Railway Station. The third level is something akin to the narrator's imagination. It is a journey back in time, an intersection of time and space. It is seen as Charley's medium of escape from the pulls and pressures of life.

The story is a masterpiece by Jack Finney, a writer of science fiction who describes the 'Third Level' as a mysterious world that is somewhere between our unfulfilled desires, expectations and dreams. It is a point of no escape where the time dimension (the past, present and future) does not exist.

The Story Retold

Three levels at the Grand Central Railway Station

The narrator feels that there are three levels at the Grand Central Railway Station. In reality, there are only two. He has discussed this with his psychiarist friend, Sam Weiner. Sam feels that the narrator's experience is a waking-dream wish fulfilment. The psychiarist says that he (the narrator) is unhappy and the modern man is engulfed in insecurities and fears. So, man wants an escape from his stressful life.

Narrator's hobby of stamp collection; a refuge

The narrator's psychiarist friend says that the narrator's hobby of stamp collection is a 'temporary refuge from reality.' The narrator does not agree with this interpretation. He argues that his grandfather lived in 'nice and peaceful' times and if this was the case his grandfather did not need to run away from reality. Still his grandfather pursued philately (the collection and study of postage stamps).

Charley reaches 'The Third Level'

One summer night Charley worked late at the office. In a hurry to get back home, he decided to take the subway from Grand Central. He crossed the arched doorway heading for the subway and got lost. The narrator strongly feels that the Grand Central grows like a tree and pushes out new corridors and stairs like roots. The narrator walks down a corridor. He finds nobody but hears empty sound of his own foot steps. He founds himself at the third level at Grand Central Station!

Scenario at 'The Third Level'

There were smaller rooms, fewer ticket windows and open-flame gaslights here. The information booth was made of wood and was looking ancient. Everybody at the station was dressed in the fashion of the late 19th century. To be sure, the narrator got a copy of 'The World' dated June 11, 1989 where the lead story was about President Cleveland.

The narrator goes to the ticket window and demands two tickets for Galesburg, Illinois. He wants to go there with his wife, Louisa. He imagines it to a peaceful countryside in the year 1894 when the First World War was twenty years away and the Second World War was forty years away. To his surprise, the clerk at the ticket counter does not accept his currency bills. Sensing trouble, the narrator runs away from the third level to escape jail.

Charley buys old currency

The narrator withdraws three hundred dollars from the bank next day to buy the currency of 1890. His psychiarist friend is really worried over this. However, his three hundred dollars got reduced to two hundred in old-style bills. He doesn't care because he desperately wants to reach the third level.

Quest for 'The Third Level'

The narrator fails to find the third level again. His wife is very worried and pursues Charley to stop looking for the third level. So, he resumes his hobby of stamp collection. His psychiarist friend, Sam disappears and the narrator and his wife get proof of the existence of the third level. Now both of them start their futile search for the third level platform. The narrator believes the Sam is now is Galesburg in the year 1894.

The mystery of first-day covers

When a new stamp is issued, stamp collectors buy it and affix a new stamp on an envelope. They mail the envelope to themselves on the first day of the sale. The postman gives proof of the date. The envelope is never opened and nothing is written inside it. This is called first day cover.

While finnicking with his stamp collection, the narrator finds a strange cover mailed to the narrator's grandfather's address in Galesburg. It has been present there since July 18, 1894. It bears a six cent stamps with the picture of President Garfield. The envelope contains a letter for Charley by his friend Sam. Sam confirms the presence of the third level and advises the narrator to keep looking for it. He says 'It's worth it.

Narrator's reality check on Sam

Charley finds out that Sam had bought eight hundred dollars worth of old-style currency. This money was sufficient to set up a hay, feed and grain business which Sam dreamt of Sam is a qualified psychiarist but cannot go back to his profession in Galesburg of 1894 because the profession of psychiarists did not exist at that time.

Exercises

Read and find out   (Page 1)

Question 1. What does 'The Third Level' refer to?

Answer 'The Third Level' symbolizes man's innermost and deepest desire to escape from the world full of tensions, war, insecurity and fear. It stands for man's pursuit of quest for a life full of peace and tranquility in contrast to the materialistic and self centred world of today.

Read and find out   (Page 5)

Question 2. Would Charley ever go back to the ticket-counter on the third level to buy tickets to Galesburg for himself and his wife?

Answer No, Charley couldn't buy two tickets from the ticket-counter on the third level for his wife and himself. When the clerk is surprised to see different kinds of notes in Charley's hand, he turns away and goes out fast to buy old currency notes, but he never finds the corridor that leads to the third level at the Grand Central.

Reading with insight   (Page 7)

Question 1. Do you think that the third level was a medium of escape for Charley? Why?

Answer The modern world is full of fear, insecurity, war, worry and stress. Man feels bogged down and helpless. He does not understand what to do and how to come out of adverse circumstances. So, he looks for a 'temporary refuge from reality'.

Charley, belonging to the twentieth century faced the same dilemma of a modern man. Busy in the rut of life, he indulged in his hobby of stamp collection for some mental peace and tranquility. Undoubtedly, it was always in his subconscious mind to find a means of escape from the ironies and materialistic bent of the world. Moreover, he had an earnest desire for things 'pretty, nice and peaceful', as they were in his grandfather's time. Then when he meets his psychiatrist he admits that 'everybody I know wants to escape'.

All these things combined together resulted in his flight of fancy to the third level. Sam, the psychiatrist also told him that his claim was 'a waking dream wish fulfilment'. Hence we can say, that the third level was a medium of escape.

Question 2. What do you infer from Sam's letter to Charley?

Answer Sam's letter was found in the oldest first day covers of Charley's grandfather. It was dated July 18, 1894 and was written from Galesburg, Illinois. This means that Sam had found the third level and escaped.

Although he diagonsed Charley's problem as an escape from life, he himself had been bothered by the humdrum existence and frustrations. In the letter, he asks Charley and Louisa to keep looking for the third level as 'It's worth it'. Sam always wanted a tranquil, easy going, pleasurable life in the countryside and wished to set up a hay and grain business.

The reader is not surprised by Sam's letter to Charley but instinctively feels that how come the letter was found in an old first-day cover in grandfather's collection? How come it was addressed to Charley and not to his grandfather although the address on the envelope was of the grandfather? Moreover, like the third level, it is possible that the letter could be a figment of Charley's imagination. Thus, the letter gives an interesting angle to the story and makes the reader curious.

Question 3. "The modern world is full of insecurity, fear, war, worry and stress." What are the ways in which we attempt to overcome them?

Answer   The modern world, undoubtedly makes us frustrated, helpless and overworked. Our subconscious mind thus, finds ways and means to escape tensions.

Depending on our upbringing, mindset and interests, people find novel ways to overcome such a sorry state of affairs. Most people find refuge in hobbies. The narrator, Charley, indulges in stamp collection to break the monotony of his life and use time productively.

Many turn to yoga, religion, spirituality, exercise, books, music and creative fields like painting and writing to overcome stress and find time for themselves.

These interests help reduce stress, anxiety and hopelessness associated with life. A positive energy exudes from the body making one calm, relieved and tranquil. Many health problems can be cured if we indulge in pleasurable activities.

Question 4. Do you see an intersection of time and space in the story "The Third Level"?

Answer   Yes, there is an intersection of time and space in the story. Time and space have been reduced to nothingness as all barriers related to them are broken. Charley bumps into the third level of 1894 and returns to the twentieth century. Similarly, Sam reaches Galesburg in 1894 and still can contact Charley in the twentieth century, which convincingly brings about an intersection.

Question 5. Apparent illogicality sometimes turns out to be a futuristic projection. Discuss.

Answer   Some things in life do not have a valid explanation or scientific reason. The sudden discovery of the third level by the narrator and his earnest desire to live a peaceful and contented life at Galesburg is not open to justification. The disappearance of his psychiatrist friend Sam is equally perplexing.

Both these individuals wish to escape from the insecurities and intricacies of life. They want to lead an easy going life, wayback in 1894 when no one had heard about world wars. This indicates that, because people are unhappy in their present life this can lead to frustration and eventually a virtual breakdown of emotions, relationships, organizations and systems in the future.

The other way of explaining this statement is that all inventions, sometimes or the other have been termed illogical. The cell phones we use today were an improbability some years before, but today they have become a necessity. Who knows the idea of going back in time, travelling back and forth in time (as depicted in the story) would become possible one day!

Question 6. Philately helps keep the past alive. Discuss other ways in which this is done. What do you think of the human tendency to constantly move between the past, the present and the future?

Answer The time dimension is divided into the past, the present and the future. Our past shapes our present. Similarly, in the present, lie seeds of the future. Philately helps keep the past alive. In the same way, hobbies like coin collection, books on varied topics, archaeological excavations, monuments, relics from the bygone era, movies, paintings and even music prevent our glorious past from being lost.

The human tendency to constantly move between the past, the present and the future shows man's dissatisfaction with life and a need to rationalize. We hanker after something which we do not get. The present does not leave man satisfied. He longs for the past to come back and waits incessantly for something positive to turn up in the future. While waiting for the future we torture ourselves continously in the present. We are anxious and insecure in the present, thinking about our future.

2

The Tiger King

Kalki

Introduction

Written in a quick paced narrative, the story is a satire on the conceit of those in power and authority. The 'Tiger King' dominates his subjects and people but is fearful of the British. Arrogant and obstinate, he chooses to refute the predictions of the astrologers but destiny has other plans. Finally, the prediction made when the king was an in fant proves true. The story makes an interesting read with the elements of humour, irony and the supernatural interspersed in it.

The Story Retold

The Maharaja of Pratibandapuram

Adorned with many titles, his name has been shortened to the 'Tiger King'. In a lighter vein, the author informs the readers that the Tiger King is dead. The astrologers predict that the newly born prince will become a warrior of warriors and a great hero but one day will have to meet his death.

Ten-day-old prince addresses the astrologers

The baby prince tells the astrologers that "all those who are born will one day have to die". He is cross with the astrologers and wants to know about the manner of his death. The astrologer tells him that death will come in the form of a tiger because he is born in the hour of the Bull and that the Bull and the tiger are enemies. As royalty runs in blood so does arrogance and then the infant prince warns "Let tigers beware!".

The childhood and coronation of the prince

Like other princes in India, the prince was given milk of an English cow, taught by an English tutor, looked after by English nanny and watched English films. He was crowned at the age of twenty.

Maharaja kills the first tiger; astrologer insists prediction is right

The astrologer's prediction slowly comes to Maharaja's ears. He goes on a hunting expedition and kills his first tiger. He exactingly and arrogantly told the astrologer about the killing. The Maharaja is told by the astrologer that he should be wary of the hundredth tiger and no harm will come to him till the killing of ninety-nine tigers. If the king succeeds in killing the hundredth tiger, the astrologer promises to leave his profession and cut his hair short giving the hint that it would result in the Maharaja's death.

Maharaja's tiger; killing expedition starts

Tiger hunting is banned in the state and only the Maharaja can kill tigers. A proclamation is issued that the defaulter's wealth and property would be confiscated. The Maharaja is so obsessed with tiger killing that he vows to attend to all other matters only when he achieves his ambition of killing a hundred tigers. During the course of his mission, he comes face to face with many dangerous situations. Sometimes he even fought the beast with his bare hands but each time the Maharaja was successful.

The British officer's visit; the king is caught in a tight spot

A high ranking British officer who is found of tiger-hunting visits Pratibandapuram. He wishes to go on a tiger hunting expedition. He is fond of clicking photographs with the tigers he has shot. The Maharaja refuses permission. He believes that granting the officers request would lead to further requests by other British officers.

Just because the Maharaja refused permission, he stood in danger of losing his kingdom. The Maharaja and his *dewan* decide to send samples of expensive diamond rings of different designs to the wife of the officer. The Maharaja sends samples of the fifty diamond rings to the officer's wife expecting that she would chose one or two rings but the greedy officer's wife keeps all the rings and sends thanks to the Maharaja. These rings cost the king three lakh rupees but his kingdom is saved.

Tiger hunting continues; king marries again to achieve target

Within ten years the king was able to kill seventy tigers. This resulting in the tiger population becoming extinct in the kingdom. The king tells his dewan that thirty tigers still remained to be killed. He asks him to find a suitable prince of royal family in some neighbouring kingdom with a large number of tigers.

The Maharaja kills five to six tigers during each visit to his in-laws. He manages to kill twenty nine more tigers. Thus ninety nine tiger skins adorn the walls of the reception hall in the Pratibandapuram palace. Now only one tiger remained to be killed.

The Maharaja is anxious at not finding the hundredth tiger

The tiger farms even in his father-in-law's kingdom run dry. It became impossible to locate tigers anywhere. The Maharaja recalls the astrologer's warning that he should be wary of killing the hundredth tiger.He decides to give up tiger hunting all together after achieving the target.

During this time the Maharaja receives a sudden news about the presence of a tiger near a village. It turns out to be false and in anger the king terminates the services of many officials. He orders that the villagers should be punished by doubling the land tax. The dewan warns him against taking such a drastic measure.

Dewan's role in the killing of hundred tiger

The king is thoroughly frustrated and orders the dewan to resign or find a tiger. The dewan gets worried and brings the tiger brought from People's Park in Madras and kept hidden in his house. He and his wife drag the old and emaciated tiger into the car. They take the tiger to the forest where the Maharaja is adamant on hunting. Initially the tiger is hesitant but he wanders in the Maharaja's presence. The Maharaja takes the aim and shoots the tiger. Filled with jubilation, the Maharaja orders the tiger to be brought to the capital in a grand procession.

In actuality; the tiger is not dead

The weak tiger faints from the shock of a bullet whizzing past him. Laters the hunters take a closer look of the tiger, it wakes up as if he was in a deep slumber. Shocked, the hunters fear for their lives and decide not to tell the Maharaja the truth. They kill the tiger themselves and take him in a grand procession to the town. The tiger is buried and a tomb is erected over it.

The birthday present for the three-year-old prince

After achieving his set target, the king turns his attention towards his son. He brings a wooden tiger from a toy shop and presents it to his son. The badly carved toy has a rough surface and slivers of wood stood up like quills all over it. The Maharaja while playing with the prince gets hurt when a tiny sliver pierces his right hand.He neglects the injury and pulls the sliver out.

The prophecy comes true

The wound develops pass which spreads all over the arm. Three surgeons come from Madras but fail to save the king's life. Thus, the hundredth tiger finally takes his revenge upon the 'Tiger king'.

Exercises

Before you read   (Page 8)

Question 1.   What is the general attitude of human beings towards wild animals?

Answer   The general attitude of human beings towards wild animals is that of fear because of their ferociousness and tendency to harm humans. But some people exploit them by caging or hunting them for the sadistic pleasure they derive from their 'feats', or kill them to earn money from their body parts and skins. Yet, there are people who understand the importance of sustaining ecological balance, preserving the beauty of nature and they believe in every creature's right to exist. They spread awareness about the importance of wildlife and the necessity of saving it from extinction.

Read and find out   (Page 8)

Question 1.   Who is the Tiger King? Why does he get that name?

Answer   The Tiger King was known as Sir Jilani Jung Jung Bahadur. He took many titles like His Highness Jamedar-General, Khiledar-Major, MAD, ACTC or CRCK. He was called the Tiger King because of his obssession for going on a hunting spree just to disprove an astrological prophecy. Moreover, he was as brave, as ferocious as a tiger.

(Page 10)

Question 2. What did the royal infant grow up to be?

Answer When the royal infant grew up, he proved the prediction right made for him which stated that he would be hero of heroes and champion and champions. He grew up to be a tall and strong man. At the age of twenty, the state came into his hands. With good training and nourishment, he grew up to be a good hunter and marksman.

(Page 13)

Question 3. What will the Maharaja do to find the required number of tigers to kill?

Answer The Maharaja had become so passionate about hunting the required number of tigers that he could probably go to any extent to fulfill his target. His tiger hunt continued successfully for 10 years in which he killed 70 tigers. After that the tiger population in his kingdom became extinct. Then, he decided to marry in the royal family of a state with a large tiger population. Things went as per the plan and the right match was found for the Maharaja and he was thus able to kill 99 tigers.

(Page 14)

Question 4. How will the Maharaja prepare himself for the hundredth tiger which was supposed to decide his fate?

Answer The Maharaja was very anxious to kill the hundredth tiger which was supposed to decide his fate, as he was successful in killing 99 tigers. No one knew that it would be so difficult to find the last one because now nowhere even a single tiger could be found. Realizing the gravity of the situation the Dewan arranged for the hundredth tiger from the People's Park in Madras and planted that tiger where the Maharaja was hunting.

(Page 15)

Question 5. What will now happen to the astrologer? Do you think the prophecy was indisputably disproved?

Answer As per the presentation, it was observed that the King has killed the hundredth tiger but actually it had just fainted by the noise of the shooting gun, which was later actually killed by the hunter to prove the situation correct. Therefore, no harm will be done to the astrologer because his prophecy at last proved to be correct. The King lost his life due to a tiger but this time it was a wooden tiger and hundredth in number.

Reading with insight   (Page 17)

Question 1. The story is a satire on the conceit of those in power. How does the author employ the literary device of dramatic irony in the story?

Answer In English Literature, dramatic irony is a literary device whereby the words and actions of the characters of a work of literature have a different meaning for the reader than they do for the characters. This is the result of the reader having a greater knowledge than the characters themselves. The character acts in a opposite way to the actual circumstances or the fate.

Kalki effectively uses the tool of dramatic irony in the story. Several instances in the story prove this. For example, after killing the first tiger, the Tiger King is immensely pleased. Conceited as he is, he displays it ostentatiously in front of the astrologer. But the astrologer warns him to be 'very careful with the hundredth tiger'. The King goes on a killing spree and in this manner gets rid of ninety-nine tigers. Having shot at the hundredth tiger, the King believes that now no harm can come to him. But the reader, the King's officers and his sycophants come to know that the lamb like tiger had only fainted from the shock of a bullet.

In jubilation, the King conveniently believes that he had belied the prediction and is willfully ignorant of what lies in store for him. A sliver on the wooden tiger's body, that is a present for the prince causes his death. Thus, the astrologer's prediction finally comes true.

Kalki's work is a powerful satire on the royalty of yesteryears who went by their own whims and fancies. The cruel behaviour of the Tiger King with the animals was just to prove the astrologer's prediction wrong shocks and surprises the readers.

Question 2. What is the author's indirect comment on subjecting innocent animals to the willfulness of human beings?

Answer The author wants to tell his readers that killing innocent animals for one's whims and wishes is wrong and sinful. The Tiger King goes on a hunting spree just to prove that he is all powerful and to disprove a mere prediction. Every living being has the right to live his life. The Tiger King interferes in the natural course of nature by indulging in the heinous slaughter of tigers.

It is ironic that fate has other plans for a conceited man like him. The Tiger King does not honour the right to live of other beings. Fate pays him in the same coin by awarding him death through a wooden tiger! The surgeons who perform the operation seem to be hammering in the point that death is common to all. Riches and power cannot help us escape death.

The surgeons seem to question the very authority of the king. Being the master of a piece of land does not mean that he can take away another's life. The Tiger King was acting like a demigod by subjecting others to his whims and fancies but when it comes to himself he could not do anything.

Thus, the author wants to drive home the point that all of us are subject to decay. Death is common to all and all beings have the right to live life, we are nobody to take away other's lives. The Tiger King breaks the divine law and so is severely punished by the divine powers for his misdeeds.

Question 3. How would you describe the behaviour of the Maharaja's minions towards him? Do you find them truly sincere towards him or are they driven by fear when they obey him? Do we find a similarity in today's political order?

Answer Conceited, ruthless, cruel and driven by whims and fancies, the Maharaja belongs to the typical ruling class in India. Devoid of any logic or reasoning powers, the Maharaja is happy when he comes to know about the presence of the hundredth tiger in a village. He doubles the taxes of the village when the tiger cannot be traced. The Maharaja's minions including his dewan are subservient to him. They are sycophants. Although he is an adviser to the Maharaja, he knows that going against him can have disastrous consequences. So, the dewan supports his marriage to a princess whose kingdom has a sizable tiger population. When the hundredth tiger could not be found, the dewan plants a tiger for the Maharaja to shoot just to save his skin.

When the king missed his mark, his minions kill the emaciated tiger themselves to save their jobs. They even take out a procession as per the instructions given by the Maharaja. None of his minions want to incur his wrath by going against him. Even the shopkeeper quotes a high price for the wooden tiger as he knows his failure to do so can make him an offender under the laws of emergency.

Undoubtedly, it is fear and authority that make the minions work for the King. They are insincere and pretend to be utterly loyal to him. Actually, they all have their own selfish ends. They are cowards and fear they would be thrown out if they are lot subservient towards the Maharaja. The situation in the present times is the same. Everybody has their own axe to grind. Nobody is working for the welfare of the country. Lies, injustice and greed reign supreme. No one is bothered about the greater good.

Question 4. Can you relate instances of game-hunting among the rich and the powerful in the present times that illustrate the callousness of human beings towards wildlife?

Answer In the times of erstwhile, Rajas and Maharajas hunting ferocious and wild animals like the tiger, the rhino, the bison et al was a sport. They proudly displayed them in their palaces as trophies. Game hunting was a way of life among the rich. When democratic governments came to power and the royals were stripped of their titles, voices were raised against the indiscriminate killing of wild animals for nothing but sport. After all it is important to preserve our natural heritage, and diverse flora and fauna. Wildlife acts were passed and stringent laws were made to stop the ruthless slaughter. Even then it was felt that the poor were being caught and the rich were allowed to go scotfree.

In the recent times, however, wildlife laws have been strictly enforced. No leverage is being given even to people with pulls and pressure. A Bollywood star known for his physique was in news for killing black buck in Rajasthan during the shooting of a film there. The black buck is a rare species and is covered under the wildlife act. Another instance is of a former test cricket captain and ruler of an erstwhile state.

These instances illustrate insensitivity towards wildlife. It is because of such carelessness and callous attitude that our national animal, the tiger, is on the verge of extinction.

Question 5. We need a new system for the age of ecology – a system which is embedded in the care of all people and also in the care of the Earth and all life upon it. Discuss.

Answer   Being the finest creation of God, man on the basis of his intelligence has dominated all other forms of life on earth.

In a bid to satisfy his innumerable needs, man has altered the symbiotic relationship between him and nature. Man's needs have changed into greed now. It is said that, 'the earth has enough for man's need but not enough to satisfy his greed'. This has led to a dismal scenario where we have to face problems like global warming, melting polar ice-caps, receding glaciers, soil erosion, pollution, depleting forest cover and extinction of several species of flora and fauna.

It is surprising that when man indulges in such mindless activities he does not think even for an instant that his own survival is on tenterhooks. It is important that at this critical juncture, we need a revolution to save our planet and its ecological heritage. We need to put immediate checks on industrial activities, increase the forest cover and let our Earth remain green.

The bourgeoning population growth needs to be curbed. Food stocks need to be built and bio fuels need to be encouraged. We must understand that we need to conserve our resources. The Earth at this stage can only hold a limited number of people with its finite resources. We must find out ways to replenish them and check their depleting cover. It requires Herculean efforts but for the safety of our blue planet it is worth a try.

3

Journey to the End of the Earth

Tishani Doshi

Introduction

This is an enlightening account of Tishani Doshi's visit to the coolest, windiest, driest continent in the world. She is hopeful that this vast expanse of ice will unlock many mysteries about the evolution of Earth. Her in-depth knowledge of Antarctica, its geography and environment is incredible.

The Story Retold

The journey to Antarctica begins

The narrator heads towards Antarctica aboard *'Akademic Shokalskiy'*, a Russian research vessel with a group of high school students. She reveals that Antarctica is the coldest, driest and windiest continent in the world. She commences her journey from Madras, crosses nine time zones, six checkpoints, three water bodies and many ecospheres to reach her destination. Travelling over hundred hours, she feels relief and wonders about the isolation of the continent and the historic time when India and Antarctica were a part of the same landmass.

Gondwana and the shaping of the modern world

The narrator takes the reader back to six hundred and fifty million years. At that time, Antarctica was a part of a giant amalgamated Southern supercontinent called Gondwana.

At that time humans had not arrived. The climate as warm and there was a huge variety of flora and fauna. For around 500 million years Gondwana existed. Eventually the landmass broke up and was forced to separate into countries. This shaped our present globe.

Narrator wonders at Antarctica; finds it blissful

Belonging to a relatively warm country, the narrator who is a South Indian is shocked to be in place where 90% of the Earth's total ice volumes are stored! She feels she's walking into a giant ping-pong ball. There is no human life there and nothing to show that human life exists on this planet. She is surrounded by midges, mites, blue whales and limitless expanse of huge icebergs. The surreal twenty four-hour summer lights and eerie silence that is interrupted only by the breaking of an iceberg, is mind-boggling.

Human impact on the environment

Human beings have been on the Earth for about 12000 years. In this short span of time we have changed the face of our environment for worse. We have dominated the Earth by establishing cities and megacities. This has led to encroachment of Mother Nature. We are limiting resources on the planet for other creatures. Burgeoning population has added to our woes. The average global temperature is rising and the blanket of carbon dioxide around the world is increasing.

The paradox of climate change

There are many unanswered questions about climate change and the narrator is alarmed by them.

Will the West Antarctic ice sheet melt entirely?

Will the gulf stream ocean current be disrupted?

Will the world come to on end?

In this debate, Antarctica has a major role to play. This is because as compared to other places it remains relatively 'pristine' and contains half-million-years-old carbon records trapped in its layers of ice. The Earth's past, present and future lies hidden in Antarctica.

'Students on ice' programme

This programme aims at studying the ecological processes in Antarctica. The narrator works on this project on board *'Akademik Shokolskiy'*, It takes school students on the trip of Antarctica. The visit aims at generating a new awareness and respect for our planet in young, impressionable minds.

The programme has been in operation for six years. It is headed by a Canadian, Geoff Green. Earlier he used to take celebrities, retired rich and curiosity seekers to Antarctica for money. Gradually he got sick of those people who gave nothing to the Earth in return. So, he decided to take school students there. It was his firm belief that young minds could learn and act better about the potential hazards regarding the environment which our Earth faces.

The programme was a success because children could see with their own eyes collasping ice shelves and retreating glaciers. They realised that the threat of global warming was real.

Lessons to be learnt

The greatest lesson to be learnt is little changes in the environment can have big repercussions. The microscopic phytoplankton are nourishment for marine animals and birds in the region. Any more depletion in the ozone layer will affect the activities of these grasses. This will in turn affect the lives of others in this region and the global carbon cycle. The phytoplankton leads us to conclude that if we take care of small things, the big things can be saved.

A memorable walk on the ocean

The narrator says that the experience of strolling on the ocean at Antarctica was a never-to-be-forgotten incident for all. At 65.55 degrees South of equator, the narrator and the students were told to get down. They put on Gore-Tex ice shoes and Sun glasses. On over 180 metres of salt water, there was one metre thick layer of ice. It was a breathtaking experience to see crabeater seals sitting in the periphery. It was truly a memorable experience for all.

The difference the Antarctic trip made

The author is overwhelmed with the beauty of balance in play on our planet. She has many questions in her *e.g.,* what would happen if Antarctica becomes a warm place ? Will human beings survive on Earth ? Whatever be the answers to these questions, she is full of optimism about the teenagers who are full of idealism to save the Earth after having made the trip of Antarctica.

Exercises

Before you read (Page 19)

Question 1. How do geological phenomena help us to know about the history of humankind?

Answer It is the geological phenomena that truly lets us know about the history of humankind, as they present before us how things were and how they evolved and many went to extinction. 650 million years ago a giant southern super continent Gondwana existed. It centered roughly around present day Antarctica. Human beings hadn't arrived on the global scene. There was a huge variety of flora and fauna. After 500 million years, the landmass was forced to separate into countries as they exist today.

Read and find out (Page 20)

Question 2. What are the indications for the future of humankind?

Answer Keeping the present condition in mind, the future of humankind is in dark and a matter of grave concern. Rapid growth of human population, limited resources and depletion of ozone layer due to disturbed global carbon cycle are severe warnings for humans as well as sea animals and birds of the region. There are many reasons responsible for the present condition but severe and immediate attention can probably reduce the disaster if not cure it.

Reading with insight (Page 23)

Question 1. 'The world's geological history is trapped in Antarctica'. How is the study of this region useful to us?

Answer Six hundred and fifty million years ago, Antarctica was a giant amalgamated landmass Gondwana. This southern supercontinent surrounded Antarctica. Human life was non-existent then. Our civilization is merely 12000 years old. The climate then was quite warm and the landmass was covered with a large variety of flora and fauna.

At a later stage, when the dinosaurs got wiped off and mammals began to appear, the landmass disintegrated and countries like, India the Himalayas and the South America were formed and got fixed in their present position. This left Antarctica cold and desolate at the bottom of the Earth.

Today, Antarctica holds key to the significance of Cordilleran folds and pre-Cambrian granite shields, ozone and carbon layers as well as evolution and extinction. It can help us understand the formation of continents and mountains like the Himalayas as we find them in the modern world.

Its ice-cores hold over half-million-year old carbon records which are crucial for the study of the Earth's past, present and future. Thus, Antarctica is the place to go to understand, the Earth's past, present and future.

Question 2. What are Geoff Green's reasons for including high school students in the Students on Ice expedition?

Answer Growing children are the future and that is the reason why Geoff Green decided to include high school students in the expedition. At this stage, it would be easier for them to grasp things and realize the impact of nature in a more demonstrative manner. The idea is to foster a new understanding and respect for our planet. Inspiring educational opportunities could be discovered by them. Antarctica provided young students a perfect place to study the changes in the environment as these changes can have big repercussions. The entire expedition was a life changing experience for the young learners where they were taught to learn, absorb and act.

Question 3. 'Take care of small things and the big things will take care of themselves.' What is the relevance of this statement in the context of the Antarctica environment?

Answer Phytoplanktons are single-celled plants that nourish and sustain the entire Southern Ocean's food chain. Scientists are of the view that a further depletion in the ozone layer will affect the activities of phytoplankton. This will adversely affect the lives of all the marine animals and birds of the region, and the global carbon cycle. These grasses give us a very insightful lesson, *i.e.*, it is important to take care of small things to save big things.

Question 4. Why is Antarctica the place to go to, to understand the Earth's present, past and future?

Answer Around six hundred and fifty million years ago, the present day Antarctica was the part of a giant amalgamated southern supercontinent called Gondwana. At this time, human beings had not yet evolved and the climate was warm. A huge variety of flora and fauna adorned the earth. For 500 million years, Gondwana existed but soon the landmass was forced to disintegrate into countries like India with the Himalayas, the roof of the world. South America drifted towards North America which resulted in Antarctica moving down below to the South Pole.

Today, Antarctica is to unlock the mystery behind the formation of Cordilleran folds and pre-Cambirian granite shields. It can help us understand the carbon and ozone layers possibly in a better way. All mindless talk about evolution and extinction can come to a standstill because Antarctica has witnessed all this.

This part of the Earth remains relatively 'pristine', it has never sustained a human settlement. Its ice-cores hold half-million year-old carbon records trapped in innumerable layers of ice. These can give us the much needed headway to study and examine the Earth's past, present and future. This is why Tishani Doshi belives that Antarctica is the place where we could 'get a grasp of where we have come from and where we could possibly be heading'.

4

The Enemy

Pearl S Buck

Introduction

'The Enemy' by Pearl S Buck is a heart rending potrayal of the conflict between man's head and heart. it is an anti-war story that highlights man's essential goodness and universal brotherhood.

With the Second Word War as its background, the story through the character of Dr Sadao Hoki questions jingoism and insane nationalism. Dr Sadao performs his duty of saving a human life first. The author condemns war in a subtle tone, never sounding didactic. Although Japan is at war with America, there is a world beyond the narrow confines of patriotism. It is the world of sympathy and kindness which is effectively brought out through the author's artistic sketches of Tom, the POW and Sadao as well as his wife Hana, who take a humanistic view of the situation.

The Story Retold

Dr Sadao Hoki's childhood

As a child, Dr Sadao lives in a house on a Japanese coast. He often played there as a small boy. The house was set upon rocks above a narrow beach. As a child Sadao used to climb pine trees on the beach. He often visited the South sea Islands with his father and had a great regard for him. His father believed the Island to be stepping stones to Japan's future. His father was a serious and quiet man. He never joked or played with his son. His son's education was his chief concern so at twenty-two Sadao was sent to America to study surgery and medicine.

Sadao comes back; is retained in Japan

Sadao became a known surgeon and scientist when he returned to Japan. At that time he was thirty years old. He achieved fame when his father was still alive. Sadao then was perfecting a discovery which would render wounds clean.

He was not sent with the troops during the Second World War because, the old General was not keeping well. At any time Sadao's services could be needed. So, Sadao was ordered to be in Japan.

How Sadao met Hana in America?

While Sadao was musing about, watching the mists around the Island over the shore, he saw Hana wearing haori over kimono. She opened the door and affectionately stood near him.

Sadao recalls his stay in America. He met Hana accidentally at an American professor's house. He liked her at first sight but his father's liking for everything Japanese restrained him. Sadao's regard for his father's patriotism forced him to wait until he was sure that Hana is Japanese. In America, Sadao lived in Professor Harley's house. They were kind people but he hated the food and small rooms. He disliked the professor's voluble wife.

Sadao and Hana's marriage

When Sadao returned to Japan, his father approved of their marriage. The marriage was arranged in the traditional Japanese style. Both of them were delighted with the marriage and enjoyed the conjugal bliss perfectly.

A stranger in the sea

While both of them were enjoying the view they saw something black coming out of the mists. They both leaned over the railing of the verandah and guessed it was a fisher man washed from his boat. They run down to the beach and notice a wounded, unconscious man. He is badly torn and wounded. Hana suddenly realises that it is a white man.

Both take a closer look

When the couple take a closer look they confirm that it is a white man who is unconscious. He is bleeding profusely. A gunshot wound had been reopened. The rocks had struck the wound and made its condition worse. Sadao stops the bleeding by packing the wound with sea moss. he perceives putting the stranger back into the sea and Hana agrees with him.

Sadao is caught in a tight spot

Sadao is faced with a difficult choice. He knows that giving shelter to POW is risky and could get them arrested. If he is handed over as a prisoner, he would certainly die. Sadao reiterates that 'All Americans are my enemy' but he cannot throw the stranger into the sea because he is wounded. His sense of duty to his profession and the human spirit stop him from doing such an act.

The questions of the servants trouble Sadao and they decide to tackle them by telling them of his intention of hand over the POW to the police. Both of them agree and decide to take the stranger inside their house. it seems the man has been starved for days as he is as light as a fowl. They keep him in Sadao's father's room who is dead now. Everything is of Japanese taste in the room because Sadao's father was a staunch patriot. The placing of a 'foreigner' in his room is ironical. The P O W is covered with a beautiful silken quilt.

The servant's reaction towards the stranger

They servants were really frightened with their master's act of giving shelter to the white man. The old gardener feared that if their master healed the white man, the gun and the sea would take revenge on them. Yumi, the governess refuses to wash the American. Even the promise of handing over the American to the authorities fails to convince the servants.

Hana washes wounds; Sadao decides to operate

Hana nurses the American carefully, she dislikes him but at the same time couldn't avoid him. She cleans the upper body clearly and does not turn him over for fear of hurting the wound.

Suddenly she sees Sadao with the surgeon's emergency bag and coat. He asks her to get towels as he had decided to operate. She helped him turn the stranger. Dr Sadao was completely absorbed in his work and asked her to give anaesthesia. Hana is uncomfortable when she sees the bleeding wound and runs out to vomit.

When the American starts groaning, Sadao says "I am not doing this for my own pleasure. In fact, I do not know why I am doing it."

The young man's thin face reminds Hana of the sufferings of the prisoners. At this moment she observes deep red scars on his neck and tells this to Sadao. Sadao is so involved in his work that he does not answer back.

Sadao remembers his American professor

In his pursuit of finding the bullet, Dr Sadao had to use his fingers. At this he recalls the words of his old American professor of anatomy who said, "Ignorance of the human body is the surgeon's cardinal sin, sirs!" The professor also viewed operating without the knowledge of the human body as murder.

At last he was able to find the bullet and reiterated that the young American would live.

The stranger recuperates

The young man was served by Hana because the servants refused to enter the room where he was kept. He is surprised when Hana talks to him in English. Hana tells him that her stay in America has taught her English. The POW is not liked by Hana still she comforts him. After the third day the young American feels better but is advised to lie down by the doctor. Worried about his future the American asks Sadao if he would be handed over to the police. At this Sadao was undecided.

The servants decide to leave

Hana tells Sadao that the servants feel that they cannot stay with them if the white man is concealed in their house. The servants felt that she and Sadao were so long in America that they had forgotten to think of the welfare of their own country first. They think that the couple liked the Americans.

At this Sadao emphasizes the fact that 'Americans are our enemies' but he has been trained not to let a man die if he can save him. They could sense that although the servants were courteous they were cold do their masters.

Hana overhears the servants conversation and feels they are right when they say that their master will be termed as traitor. She felt that Tom, the POW was a great trouble.

Meanwhile, Sadao went to his office and carefully typed a letter to the Chief of Police about the whole incident. But he left it unfinished. Thus, on the seventh day the servants left and Hana like a good master paid them their wages.

The General's message

Hana sees a messenger come to their house in official uniform. He tells her that Sadao has been summoned to come to the palace as the General was unwell. Hana falt relieved at this.

General's dependency on doctor

Dr Sadao was not sent to accompany the troops owing to General's illness. He frankly told the General that he could bear only one attack. The Genseral reposes full faith in the doctor and feels Dr Sadao can save anyone. He promised the doctor that he would never be sent to the front or arrested as (The general) might need an operation anytime and he had no faith in surgeons taught by the Germans.

The General's promise and Sadao's sleepless nights

When Sadao tells the General about the stranger, the General promises to send his private assassins to finish the POW. He assures him of removal of the dead body also. Sadao decides not to tell anything to Hana about it. He considers such assassins necessary in an absolute state like Japan.

The General had told Dr Sadao that his private assassins would kill the doctor any night. Being sympathetic and human, Sadao spends a sleepless night. Time and again he imagines the rustling sound of assassins approaching. The next morning he is relieved to find Tom in his room. Sadao spends two more sleepless nights waiting for the assassins.

Dr Sadao arranges Tom's escape

Sadao advises Tom, the POW to row close to the Island which was near the coast. He decides to give the POW his own boat, food and clothing. Sadao warns him not to take help of any boat except the Korean boat to go away. The doctor gives him his flashlight complete with instructions about when to use it. After Sadao saves Tom's life by making him escape, he slept peacefully.

Sadao meets the General again

Sadao tells the General about POW's escape. The General had survived another operation. He told the doctor that he was so pre-occupied with his illness that he forgot all about the assassins. Both reiterate their sense of patriotism, duty and integrity towards their country.

Sadao wonders why he couldn't kill Tom

Standing on the veranda, Sadao recalls his days in America. He thinks of the dull professor and his silly talkative wife. He remembers his old teacher of anatomy and the face of the fact landlady. He remembers all the difficulties and miseries he had to fact while living in America and the prejudiced behaviour of the Americans towards the Japanese. Finally, deep in thought, he wonders why he could not kill Tom, the American prisoner of war.

Brief Character Sketches
of the Characters in the Story

Dr Sadao's fathers

- Loves his country; a patriot.
- Called the Island in the South seas, "the stepping stones to the future of Japan".
- A serious person, 'never joked or played' with his only son.
- 'Took infinite pains' regarding son's education.
- Sent Sadao to America for advance studies in the fields of medicine, surgery and science
- Devoted to Japanese culture and tradition.
- Saw to it that Hana belonged to a 'pure' race; marriage was organised in the traditional Japanese way.
- Only had Japanese made things in his room.
- At heart a Japanese to the core

Dr Sadao Hoki

- Father's values had a great impact.
- Revered his father.
- Remembered father's words about the Islands in the South seas being "stepping stones for Japan."
- Fulfilled father's dreams, aspirations; became a renowned surgeon and scientist.
- An intellectual; was 'perfecting a discovery' aimed at rendering wounds absolutely clean.
- Adept in surgical skills.
- Regard for father compels him to wait for father's approval for Hana.
- Caring and adorable husband.
- Consults Hana on all issues; gives a patient hearing to her views.
- Vouches for her suggestion when they find the POW on the shore. Accepts her view when the servants are to be told about the America.

Wholly devoted to his profession

Remembers professor's words, "Ignorance of the human body is the surgeon's cardinal sin, sirs" and "To operate without complete knowledge of the body as if you had made it—anything less than that is murder."

- Kind-hearted, humane; spends sleepless night at the fact the General has promised to send private assassins to kill the POW.
- Saves the POW's life again by helping him escape.

Hana

- Adorable wife; perfect homemaker; good master.
- Has perfect understanding with Sadao; is consulted on all vital issues by him.
- When Yumi, the governess refuses to wash the POW she is troubled; feels he is 'a wounded helpless man'.
- Kind and considerate; although never ever attempted to nurse anybody when Sadao insists, she does it dexterously.
- Tensed about what to do with the POW; a conflict goes on in her mind incessantly.
- Dignified; doesn't get cross with servants or hankers after them.
- Generous, benevolent; gives servants wages there and then.

Tom; the American Prisoner of War

- A destiny's child.
- Survives the gun shot and braves the rocky sea.
- Fortunate to be washed ashore near Dr Sadao and Hana's house.
- Has been starved and tortured but still had an indomitable will to survive against all odds.
- Even Dr Sadao realises this when he says, "This man will live inspite of all" and "he has extraordinary vitality".
- After recuperating, filled with awe and terror; realises he is in Japan.
- Straightforward.
- Fearing harm asks Dr Sadao what did he intend to do with him.
- Finally escapes from enemy territory with the help of Sadao.
- His escape; a miracle.

General Takima

- Self-centered; although the Second World War is in full swing he keeps Dr Sadao available for him in case of need in Japan instead of sending him with the troops.

- Forgetful; at first commits to send the assassins but pre-occupation with illness makes him forget his promise.
- Humourous; talks about German ruthlessness; doesn't want to get operated by German trained doctors because they "would consider the operation successful, even if the patient died."
- American sentimentality interests him.
- Doesn't want anyone to doubt his integrity, patriotism towards his country.

Exercises

Before you read   (Page 24)

Question 1. It is the time of the World War. An American prisoner of war is washed ashore in a dying state and is found at the doorstep of a Japanese doctor. Should he save him as a doctor or hand him over to the Army as a patriot?

Answer As a doctor and as an individual, his first duty is to save the man by giving him the necessary medical help, as it is his ethical responsibility, whatever the risks. Later on, he should be patriotic and inform the Police or the Army about the presence of the American prisoner of war at his house, making it clear to them that the American is in a critical state.

Read and find out   (Page 24)

Question 1. Who was Dr Sadao? Where was his house?

Answer Dr Sadao was a famous and established Japanese doctor who had gone to America for learning and gaining expertise in medicine and surgery. Dr Sadao's house was beautifully located on the Japanese coast. It was a low, square stone house, set upon rocks above a narrow beach and the beach was outlined with bent pines.

Read and find out   (Page 27)

Question 2. Will Dr Sadao be arrested on the charge of harbouring an enemy?

Answer On the national front, giving shelter to an enemy is always considered to be an anti-national work, but things change when seen on personal and moral context. Japan is at war with America and Dr Sadao can be arrested and punished for harbouring an enemy. But such a thing will not happen because his servants are loyal to him and the old General who knows the matter is silent about it. Therefore, there is no proof to find Dr Sadao guilty.

Read and find out   (Page 31)

Question 3. Will Hana help the wounded man and wash him herself?

Answer It is very natural on Hana's part to have initial hesitations in helping an enemy. She is apprehensive of being arrested on giving shelter to a war prisoner. Later she overcomes her inhibitions on the grounds of humanity and obedience towards her husband who compels her to help him save Tom's life. Later she herself washes the wounded man.

Read and find out   (Page 35)

Question 4. What will Dr Sadao and his wife do with the man?

Answer Dr Sadao and his wife treated the man well enough for him to get back into senses so that he could move on and leave the place. Because he was a war prisoner they had no intention of keeping him back for long and therefore made arrangements for him to leave as soon as possible.

Read and find out   (Page 39)

Question 1. Will Dr Sadao be arrested on the charge of harbouring an enemy?

Answer It was now unlikely that Dr Sadao would be arrested on the charge of harbouring an enemy because the old General was being treated by Dr Sadao. If he was arrested, there would be no one to operate upon the General in case of an emergency. Further, Sadao had informed the General about the presence of the American in his house.

Read and find out   (Page 43)

Question 5. What will Dr Sadao do to get rid of the man?

Answer Because Dr Sadao helped the man to survive he wanted him to leave his house and reach to his destination at the earliest and the safest. Therefore, he gives him a boat with sufficient food and clothes to go to the nearby island. From there the man could take a Korean boat and escape to freedom at night.

Reading with insight   (Page 47)

Question 1. There are moments in life when we have to make hard choices between our roles as private individuals and as citizens with a sense of national loyalty. Discuss with reference to the story you have just read.

Answer   There are times when we are faced with difficult choices in life. An individual is torn apart between his duty towards his motherland and the moral responsibility of helping a needy person. This is the same dilemma that the Sadaos are confronted with.

As patriotic citizens of Japan, they are expected to hand over an American prisoner of war especially at the the time of Second World War. But this is a myopic view of the situation. If we bring in the humanistic angle to this dismal reality, then it is a doctor's duty to save a human life. As a doctor one should not differentiate between an enemy and an ally. How could Sadao leave Tom bleeding to death?

Similarly, Hana, an epitome of kindness cannot leave a wounded person ashore. When Humi, the governess decides not to wash a dirty white man she says, "Is this anything but a man? And a wounded helpless man!" Likewise Sadao goes through a tortuous mental conflict. They can't decide what to do with Tom. Although they try to act rationally (Hana even says that even the servants see more clearly then we do? Why are we different from other Japanese?") their heart rules their mind.

All the developments lead Sadao to let the prisoner of war escape safely.

Question 2.   **Dr Sadao was compelled by his duty as a doctor to help the enemy soldier. What made Hana, his wife, sympathetic to him in the face of open defiance from the domestic staff?**

Answer   As a doctor it was Dr Sadao's moral responsibility to save Tom (the American prisoner of war), but Hana was under no such compulsion. Inspite of this she endorses her husband's views because she is a dutiful wife who pledges to support her husband even through the most difficult times.

Secondly, Hana being a woman is tender hearted. She could not see a wounded person being left in a lurch. As a woman she adorns the role of a life-giver and a preserver. How can she be a destroyer?

She is educated so inspite of the domestic staff being against Tom she decides to support her husband's cause. She can think logically and hence is not affected by their chauvinism. She does not budge from her stand although she knows that the risks and stakes involved are immense.

Question 3.   **How would you explain the reluctance of the soldier to leave the shelter of the doctor's home even when he knew he couldn't stay there without risk to the doctor and himself?**

Answer   Tom, the American prisoner of war knew fully well that the Sadaos had saved his life although being Japanese citizens they could have left him to fend for himself. He is aware of their empathetic nature towards him. Moreover, he understands that the Sadaos house is a safe haven for him because they had stayed in America and can communicate with him in English easily. In an enemy country, there are foes all around and he can be subjected to torture, gun shots, the rocky sea and gallows, he feels he is in safe hands. Somewhere, it is possible, he comes to know about the influence and power that the Sadaos wield. No doubt he feels secure at their place.

Another relevant reason could be that since the house is near the beach, Tom thinks he could escape any time from there just in case the circumstances are not in his favour.

Thus, Tom senses the essential goodness of Sadao and Hana. In his heart of hearts, he is very sure that they will not hand him over to the cruel authorities who (as his scars on the neck prove) have meted out inhuman treatment to him. Being a human being, his instinct of securing himself is topmost in his mind. So, he is reluctant to leave the Sadao household.

Question 4. What explains the attitude of the General in the matter of the enemy soldier? Was it human consideration, lack of national loyalty, dereliction of duty or simply self-absorption?

Answer The author's description of the General potrays him to be on eccentric fellow much too preoccupied with his ill health and fear of death. He seems to be a cruel and callous person, who has recruited private assassins to eliminate anybody who stands in opposition to the state.

This description does not lead us to believe that he could be considerate to human lives. It is therefore, surprising that he fails to send the assassins to Sadao's house. One possible reason could be that at the time he assured Dr Sadao of eliminating the American prisoner of war, he was very ill and needed Dr Sadao's services immediately. He wanted Dr Sadao to concentrate on his health completely without bothering about the enemy. Later the General forgets his promise because he is so self absorbed with his deteriorating health that he completely forgets his promise.

Had the General been loyal he would have not forgotten his promise conveniently. His desperate efforts to prove that he is truly loyal and the lapse on his part was not dereliction of duty speaks volumes for his seriousness about the issue.

It is not the dereliction of duty, lack of patriotism, human consideration or the General's stay in the Princeton University and his positive view of American sentimentality that is responsible for his forgetfulness. In fact, his intense and selfish absorption with his illness and surgery make him forget his promise.

Question 5. While hatred against a member of the enemy race is justifiable, especially during wartime, what makes a human being rise above narrow prejudices?

Answer I think hatred against a member of the enemy race is understandable. In any case, it is not justifiable. Hatred is an instant reaction on any human being's part especially during wartime.

However, in many instances human beings rise above narrow prejudices. In this case, Dr Sadao does not think twice before stopping the bleeding. He packs the wound with moss available on the sea shore. It is his moral obligation to save a human being's life although that human being is his foe. He is not affected by the chauvinism of average Japanese citizen. Although he admits, "All Americans are my enemy" his sense of humanity and sympathy does not allow him to differentiate between man and man. He spends three sleepless nights thinking the life he has saved is in danger.

In America, he himself faced the prejudice and bitter experience of staying there, he did not want Tom (the American prisoner of war), to carry forth this impression further. By saving Tom's life, he sets a valuable precedent of Japanese hospitality, humanity and generosity. He executes his plan of escape for the American sailor deftly.

Dr Sadao takes care of the wounded American POW in the manner in which he would have treated any other wounded man. He thinks about his being an American only because he does not want his family to suffer.

Thus, Sadao rises above the narrow prejudices to become a citizen of the world, the one who is compassionate and benign towards all.

Question 6. Do you think the doctor's final solution to the problem was the best possible one in the circumstances?

Answer As a doctor, Sadao fulfilled the moral obligation of saving a human life perfectly. When the General assured Dr Sadao of sending the private assassins to eliminate the American sailor, Dr Sadao felt restless and perhaps guilty of betraying the same person whose life he had saved. After spending three sleepless nights, he finally deliberates on a flawless plan to let Tom, the American prisoner of war escape. By letting him escape, Dr Sadao proves that even if two countries are at war, the religion of humanity does not alter. Its basic tenet is saving a human life which Dr Sadao does with aplomb. In a way Dr Sadao echoes the author, Pearl S Buck's views against war and the hatred that it generates between man and man. Through Dr Sadao, the author conveys the message of universal brotherhood, peace and amity. It was indeed the best solution to the problem.

Question 7. Does the story remind you of 'Birth' by AJ Cronin that you read in Snapshots last year? What are the similarities?

Answer There is much similarity between both the stories. The two stories are about doctors who use their skill to try and save human beings who are almost dead. Both stories highlight the issues of a sense of duty, selflessness, humanitarian feelings, love and affection.

Question 8. Is there any film you have seen or novel you have read with a similar theme?

Answer This story is based on a strong sense of duty, selflessness, humanitarian gestures and love for a fellow human being. A movie with a similar theme is, 'My Name is Khan', where the protagonist saves the lives of his friends from floods, guided by a strong sense of humanity and moral duty, without fearing for his own life.

5

Should Wizard Hit Mommy?

John Updike

Introduction

Written in the story within a story format, "Should Wizard Hit Mommy?" Is an entertaining story with a serious theme-why do adults impose their viewpoints on the children? What is good parenting? Is it quashing the inquisitiveness of the child?

Jack, the father of a four year-old narrates the same story to the little girl with slight variation every time. The story is predictable, yet the child listens with rapt attention and even points out to the minor inaccuracies of her father. When the story comes to its end, she raises a difficult moral question. The father is speechless and cannot convince her of his viewpoint.

The Story Retold

The story telling sessions

Jack, the father narrated stories to his daughter, Jo in the evenings and on Saturdays for putting her to sleep. This continuous story telling session began two years ago and is mentally taxing for Jack. Now Jo has turned four. Each story that Jack narrates is a minor variation of the basic tale. It starts with a small creature, usually named Roger. This Roger has a problem and goes to the wise old owl for solving it. The owl told him to go to the Wizard who solves the problem by magic spells. When the Wizard, asks for fee, Roger has insufficient money, the Wizard shows Roger where and how more money can be found. Roger finds money, pays the fee and goes home from Boston and the family has their dinner together.

Roger Skunk; the foul-smelling protagonist

At Jo's insistence, the father, Jack narrates Roger's Skunk's story. Roger Skunk wanted to play with other woodland creatures but they would run away from him because he smelt very bad. Roger Skunk feels humiliated and hurt at their behaviour. Jack feels happy that he was telling his daughter something true which she must know. While narrating the story, he thinks of his wife who is painting furniture downstairs. He wants to help her but Jo keeps him pre-occupied.

Roger Skunk meets the wise owl; Jo's curiosity

Like earlier Rogers in the stories that Jack had narrated to his daughter, Roger Skunk visits the wise owl to find a solution to his problem. He was in tears and the owl told him to visit the Wizard.

At this the really inquisitive Jo asks her father if magic spells are real. The father tells her that they are real in stories. Jack, however, does not like her questioning attitude which had begun a month ago. As she had 'made him miss a beat in the narrative'.

Roger Skunk visits the Wizard

Guided by the owl's directions, Roger Skunk reaches the Wizard's house. The Wizard was tiny little old man with a long white beard and a blue hat. The Wizard finds Skunk foul smelling and asks him not to get too close. Skunk asks him to make him smell like roses. The Wizard chants a magic rhyme and makes Roger Skunk smell like roses. At this juncture, Jack finds in Jo's expression a reflection of his wife.

As Jack narrates the story, he refers to Roger Skunk as Roger Fish. At this Jo immediately points out his mistake. Jack continues the story. The Wizard asks Roger Skunk to give him seven pennies but Roger Skunk had only four pennies.

Skunk looks for money; is happy to be back with friends

The Wizard solves this problem also and tells and him where to find the other three pennies. He found them and gave it to the Wizard. The other creatures gathered around him because he smelled so good. Roger Skunk was very happy and rushes home. His mother finds the smell of roses awful and angrily scolds him.

Skunk, mommy visit the Wizard

Skunks's mother is angry because the Wizard has made her baby smell like roses. She wants him to alter this. The Wizard gives in and changes Skunk's odour. Now Skunk smells foul once again.

Arguments ensure between Jo and Jack

Jo desperately wants the Wizard to hit back Skunk's mommy. She feels that the mother is wrong. At this Jack says that it is his story. Jo is still unconvinced.

Jack continues the story and says that both the mother and son wait for father Skunk' s return from Boston in evening. They have a sumptuous meal.Mommy, Skunk hugs and kisses Roger to sleep. She likes the smell of baby Skunk once again.

Jo's dilemma

Roger Skunk now plays heartily with the little animals. They did not run away because gradually they got used to the foul smell and did not mind it at all.

Jo does not like the ending of the story. She doesn't like that the Wizard has been defeated by Skunk's Mommy.

She wants the Wizard to hit back the mommy 'right over the head'. The father disagrees saying that Skunk loved his mommy and that mothers are always right. He advises Jo to go to sleep.

An awkward situation for the father

He saw Clare, his wife, busy painting the furniture. Jack feels that Jo is still not asleep and warns Jo of spanking her. Clare complains of the delay in his coming down.

Jack undergoes a change of mood. He finds himself and his wife trapped in a cage. He does not want to speak to her, work with her or touch her. He feels he is caught in an ugly middle position, *i.e.*, he finds life meaningless and dull. He could not convince his four year-old daughter and earns rebuke from his wife. Life, he thinks is enveloped in uncertainties and he finds hard to accept that his little daughter, full of certitude asserts herself and forces him to change the ending of the story. He feels caught up in his utopian world of stories and the dull and meaningless world he is living in.

Exercises

Read and find out   (Page 48)

Question 1. Who is Jo? How does she respond to her father's story telling?

Answer Jo is Jack's little daughter and is nearly four years old. She is very obsessed about listening to stories at bedtime and insists to hear a new story everyday to go off to sleep. Jack does not know many stories and therefore he creates stories on his own, which are in slight variation from the basic tale. She enjoys her father's story telling and shows her interest by asking many questions related to the story.

Read and find out   (Page 53)

Question 2. What possible plot line could the story continue with?

Answer The other possible plot line could be, if Roger smelled as roses for ever because he was happy with the smell. He could now play with his friends. Because this story was being heard by a small child the ending could be positive because children love happy endings.

Read and find out   (Page 54)

Question 3. What do you think was Jo's problem?

Answer Jo did not like the ending of the story because she was a sensitive girl. Roger's mother compelled the wizard to make him smell very bad again. Jo also felt very happy when Roger had started smelling like roses. Now, she wanted her father to make a change in the story. She wanted the wizard to hit Roger's mother with his magic wand to make Roger smell bad again and upset him.

Reading with insight   (Page 55)

Question 1. What is the moral issue that the story raises?

Answer On the face of it "Should Wizard Hit Mommy?" seems to be a typical story told by a father to his daughter. But there are serious underlying themes in the story.

First of all, it raises the questions that should parents have the sole authority to decide what is best for their children? Why are children expected to follow their parents' views blindly?

In the story, Roger Skunk is a very obedient kid who is sad because he really smells bad. As a result nobody plays with him. He is hurt and humiliated. One day he gets rid of his awful smell and is readily accepted by his playmates. However, his mother is annoyed and takes him back to the wizard. She wants him to get back his original smell. She hits the wizard on the head and Roger accepts his mother's words as God's command. Other creatures gradually accept Roger with his stinking smell.

Jo, the four years old child, however, cannot accept this version of the story. She feels that the mother on her part is wrong and in return she should be hit by the wizard for being cruel and insensitive to her son. Jack, the father whose reflection is Roger Skunk, disagrees and emphasizes that his views are right. Thus, the story raises another concern about the parents authority. Should there be any limit to the parents authority? Why can't children express their views in front of their parents? Why are children's viewpoints always ridiculed or criticized? These are some of the moral issues that the story raises and which the author leaves open-ended. Another important underlying theme of the story is that should we accept ourselves as we are without thinking about others (in accordance with Roger Skunk's mother views) or try and change ourselves (adapt).

Question 2. How does Jo want the story to end and why?

Answer   Jo is an avid listener of stories. She is always aware, inquisitive and alert during the story telling sessions. Like all stories of her father this one also has a creature called Roger Skunk who has a problem. His problem is that he smells awful. As a result none of the creatures befriend him and play with him. He resolves this problem by visiting the wise, old owl who guides him to go to the wizard.

The wizard makes him smell like sweet-smelling roses but Roger Skunk's mother dislikes that. She spanks the wizard with her umbrella and demands that her son should get back his original smell. Jo had not anticipated this. She believed that the story had ended where Roger Skunk gets the aromatic smell of the roses and is happily accepted by his playmates.

Jo is shocked and surprised by the twist in the version of her father's story and this is unacceptable to her. She emphasizes that the mother is gravely wrong in getting Roger back his original smell. If her son was being happily accepted by his playmates, is it right that he should smell awful again? If Roger does not like his original smell, he has every right to alter it. Jo believes that mother Skunk should be hit by the wizard for being "stupid" enough to be insensitive to Roger Skunk's feelings.

Question 3. Why does Jack insist that it was the wizard that was hit and not the mother?

Answer   Roger Skunk's devotion and obedience to his mother is a reflection of Jack's own self. Like the protagonist in his own story, Jack venerated his mother.

Even a four year old child, Jo understands fully well that Roger Skunk's mommy should be hit because she was "stupid" but her father emphasizes with 'rare emphasis' that the mother was not stupid. She (Jo) realised, "he was defending his own mother to her, or something as odd."

Jack believes that mothers are always right and must be given unconditional love and paid respect. This is what his hero, Roger Skunk does when he accepts his mother's command. He readily agrees to smell like before. On the other hand, wizards can be hit. They are under obligation to go by the mother's words. Moreover, Jack believes that the mother was eventually proved right. Mother Skunk believed that one's natural oddities need to be accepted. One must not pretend or try to change it. This is what happens with Roger Skunk also. Ultimately the little animals of the woodland accept him heartily. Thus, Roger maintained his distinct identity by keeping his original smell. Hence, Jack insists that the wizard should be hit and not the mother.

Question 4. What makes Jack feel caught in an ugly middle position?

Answer   From the story it seems that Jack is a caring and dutiful father and an equally concerned husband. That particular Saturday Jack has two things on hand. He is supposed to tell a story to his four years old daughter for her Saturday nap and is expected to help his pregnant wife, Clare with painting the household furniture.

He believes that he will quickly complete the story and go downstairs to help Clare. Things do not go in his favour. The story takes an unusually long time because his daughter who is now growing up is inquisitive and interrupts him time and again. She even points out his mistake and makes him correct it. For example, during the course of the story, Jack refers to Roger Skunk as Roger Fish. Jo does not like it. All the time during the story, she is alert and anticipates eagerly what will happen next. She even gives her own views and suggestions to her father which he rejects vehemently. Jo does not like the ending of the story as suggested by her father.

According to Jack, Mother Skunk did not like the original smell of her baby being taken away. She spanked the wizard for being so thoughtless and wanted him to return Roger his original smell. Roger Skunk even gets his playmates with this awful smell. Jo differs on this point. She wants that Mother Skunk should be hit for her insensitive behaviour by the wizard. Roger Skunk, her hero should smell like sweet roses and play with his friends happily thereafter.

Jack does not approve of this ending but he knows that ultimately he will be coaxed to narrate the ending of Jo's choice. Throughout the story session, Jack has been worrying about Clare, her health and the baby. Clare is in no mood to relent and indirectly comments on Jack about his being late. Suddenly Jack experiences a change of mood.

He is tired, bored and dejected. He feels like doing nothing. He feels trapped in the rat race of life along with Clare. He has no desire to speak to her, work with her or touch her. Perhaps Jo's incessant questioning and her obstinate behaviour has made him remember his childhood, when he felt hurt and humiliated like Roger Skunk.

Question 5. What is your stance regarding the two endings to the Roger Skunk story?

Answer Jack's ending of the story is typical and similar to all the stories he has narrated to his four years old daughter, Jo. Each new story is a slight variation of a basic tale. A small creature usually named Roger has a problem and goes to resolve it to a wise, old owl. The owl sends him to the wizard, demands payment, gets it and Roger is happy. He plays with his friend, goes home, meets father and they have their supper. Jo is used to a happy ending where all goes smooth. She does not expect a deviation. So, when Jack says that Roger gets rid of his awful smell and is happily accepted by his playmates she feels the story is over. She strongly criticizes the fact that Roger's mother does not like him smell like roses, goes and hits the wizard for doing so. She feels that Mother Skunk is grossly wrong, inhuman and cruel in her decision to make her baby smell like before. Jo is just not ready to accept it and wants her father to change the ending.

Both the endings sound interesting and valid. However's Jack's ending is more realistic and practical. It points out to the harsh realities that one has to go through. One's love for one's near and dear ones (Roger's mother in this case) makes one give up one's wishes. If we take the case of woodland creatures, even they change their attitude with time and learn to accept Roger's awful smell. This ending is mature and in tune with his childhood experience.

As regards Jo's ending, Jo is a pampered four years old who knows nothing about injustice and suffering in this world. She believes that if change of smell can lead to Roger's acceptance than why should he not go for it? She does not understand the logic behind Roger's mother's insistence on giving him back his original smell. She feels that Mother Skunk is selfish and unfair.

If I think about myself, I believe I will support Jo's stand. Every being has the right to alter himself or herself for being accepted by the society and this is what Roger does.

I think Jack should not have been so insistent on his version of the story. Stories for children are meant for entertaining and not serving the didactic purpose. So, Jo's, ending appeals to me the most.

Question 6. Why is an adult's perspective on life different from that of a child's?

Answer The adult's view of life is different from that of a child. It is more realistic, practical and matter-of-fact. In contrast to this, the child views the world with rose-coloured glasses. It is a utopian world where there is no place for injustice, selfishness, ridicule or cruelty.

Jack, the father in the story "Should Wizard Hit Mommy?" tells a story which reflects his childhood and his relation with his mother. Jack revered his mother, so does the protagonist, Roger. Jack's ending is typical of an adult ending– sacrifice your desires for a greater cause. This is what Roger does to accommodate his mother's decision. Although in the end, he does get the rewards because the woodland creatures accept him although he still smells bad. Jo, the four years old lives in a romantic and idealistic world. She is hostile, haughty and obstinate. She wants to take revenge on Skunk's mother and wants the wizard to hit back. Jack, on the other hand, feels that the wizard deserves to be punished because he has interfered with nature's ways. He had no right to make Roger smell like roses and so Jack refutes Jo's ending.

Thus, from the above discussion, we see that both the adult's and a child's perspective are different from each other.

6

On The Face of It

Susan Hill

Introduction

'On The Face of It is a play, featuring a small boy and a physically challenged old man. It is a poigant story that deals with a sense of loss, desolation and triumph over it. Derek, a young boy of fourteen suffers from inferiority complex. He is with drawn and defiant because he has an ugly face. Mr Lamb, who is a die-hard optimist alters Derek's world view by sharing his experiences with the little boy. He gives him a new lease of life by enthusing him with a new spirit to live life to the fullest.

The Story Retold

Derek meets Mr Lamb

The play is divided into three scenes. Scene the first one opens in Mr Lamb's garden. Derek sneaks into the garden thinking that there is nobody around. He is shocked when he hears a voice which says, 'Mind the apples'. Derek is embarrassed and consequently clarifies that he thought it was an 'empty house' and he had not come to steal anything. Mr Lamb assures him that he need not be afraid of anything and he does not mind strangers entering his garden or his house. The gates are always open.

Derek (Derry) suffers from complex

Mr Lamb is surprised when Derek says with pride, "I'm not afraid. People are afraid of me." This is because one side of his face got burnt because of acid. Derek expected the old man to react like others but Mr Lamb maintains his cool and calm self. He says that he is going to make jelly out of the crab apples.

Derek does not like the change of subject. Mr Lamb, however, tries of alter his (Derek's) attitude by telling him that he is interested in 'anybody', and loves all the creatures made by God. Mr Lamb says that nothing is worthless or worthy of being discarded. Even weeds which are considered useless have their own value. Thus, Mr Lamb tries to instil positivism in Derek.

Mr Lamb is handicapped too

Mr Lamb reveals that he has got a tin leg because the real one got blown off in the war. Wherever he goes, children tease him by calling "Lamey-Lamb," but he does not bother. He wants Derek to adopt the same attitude. Derek, however, is full of bitterness against the world and his mother. Derek complains that his mother kisses him on the other side of his face. She doesn't kiss on the burnt side. Mr Lamb advises him to look at the beautiful things in the world. Derek shows some sense when he philosophises and says, "think of all those people worse off than you".

Derek feels disturbed again when he tells Mr Lamb about the conversation between two women, one of whom comments, "That's a face only a mother could love". Mr Lamb asks him if he believes everything which he hears. He advises Derek to keep his ears shut and hear only those, things he wants to hear.

The incident of a timid man narrated by Mr Lamb

Mr Lamb is reminded of his hive of bees that he has to tend to. He says that some people feel bees buzz but he believes that the bees sing. Thus, Mr Lamb wants to drive home the point that it is the attitude that shapes a man.

In the course of this conversation, Derek says that he doesn't like being near people especially when he knows that they are afraid of him. At this point, Mr Lamb narrates the story of a timid man who refused to come out of his house because he feared that he will be a victim of some fatal accident. Surprisingly, he died in his room itself because "a picture fell off the wall on his head and killed him." Mr Lamb, through his story, wanted Derek to understand that one's destiny cannot be altered with. Derek laughs at this and this is the beginning of his transformation.

Derek is reminded of the pitying attitude of his family

Mr Lamb tells Derek that he does not like curtains because they shut things out. Even Derek says that he likes to hear the sound of rain on the roof. Thus, Derek has a sensitive side too. It is only that somewhere the bitterness in him has come to the forefront. He is reminded of his family members and their sympathetic attitude which he does not like. They are always worried about what will Derek do in the future. Mr Lamb, at this juncture, has encouraging words for him. He says, "You'll get on the way you want, like all the rest." He could even be 'better' than all the rest.

Mr Lamb continues to encourage Derek. He tells him that being 'friends' doesn't mean that you know the person in and out. He considers Derek to be his friend and also tells him the significance of people. He says, "People are never just nothing, Never" and asks Derek to love all because hatred is more dangerous and humiliating than acid.

Derek shows concern for Mr Lamb

Mr Lamb tells Derek, "Everything is yours if you want", whatever belongs to him is his if he likes it.

Derek is so involved and obssessed with his handicap that he only thinks of himself. But this time, he talks about Mr Lamb and his handicap. Derek says that if Mr Lamb fell from the ladder and broke his neck, he could lie on the grass and die just in case there is nobody to help him.

Mr Lamb who is a great believer in destiny says with acceptance, "I could". At this point, Derek is worried about going home. Lamb sees the philosophical side here too and says, "People worry.'

Mr Lamb throws up a challenge for Derek

Mr Lamb now understands that he has led to Derek's transformation. He reads Derek's pulse and deliberately challenges him by saying that Derek will never come back to visit the garden. Mr Lamb's intention is to help Derek, break all barriers and complexes that retard this growth as an individual.

Derek's spirit to overcome all challenges is very strong now and he tells his mother that he will get back to Mr Lamb.

Derek's ultimate transformation

Inspite of her protestations, he goes back to Mr Lamb and his garden. He sees that Mr Lamb has fallen down from the ladder and is not responding to his voice. Probably, he is unconscious or even dead. Seeing his benefactor in this pitiable state, Derek begins to cry.

Exercises

Before you read (Page 56)

Question 1. This is a play featuring an old man and a small boy meeting in the former's garden. The old man strikes up a friendship with the boy who is very withdrawn and defiant. What is the bond that unites the two?

Answer Mr Lamb and Derry have different points of view about life. Mr Lamb has a positive view while Derry's attitude is totally negative. Although Mr Lamb and Derry are totally different, the bond that unites them is that they are both physically disabled or disfigured. Both are made fun of by various people. Mr Lamb has a tin leg because he has lost one leg in a war and people make fun of him due to this. Even then, he does not change his positive thinking towards life. He lived his life to the fullest.

On the other hand, the boy Derry has a disfigured face due to acid having fallen on one side of it. Derry's burnt face makes him want to run away from society. But when he meets Mr Lamb, he gets to know how one should live one's life, because it is very precious. This change in Derry also helps him to create a bond with Mr Lamb. This common predicament has united them.

Read and find out (Page 56)

Question 1. Who is Mr Lamb? How does Derry get into his garden?

Answer Mr Lamb is an old man who lives in a big house and has a garden of his own. One of his legs was blown off in the war due to which he has a tin leg. Derry climbs over the garden wall and gets inside Mr Lamb's garden to pick up apples because he likes the place but thinks that nobody resides there.

Read and find out (Page 62)

Question 2. Do you think all this will change Derry's attitude towards Mr Lamb?

Answer Derry does not know much about Mr Lamb till he discovers it on his own. His mother prevents him from meeting Mr Lamb but he insists to carry forward because his company had changed his attitude towards life. Mr Lamb motivates him to think positively about life, people and things. He takes him out of his complex feeling of having a burnt face and instils a new vision in him which has a deep impression on his mind.

Reading with insight

(Page 69)

Question 1. What is it that draws Derry towards Mr Lamb inspite of himself?

Answer Derry enters Mr Lamb's garden stealthily. He is startled when Mr Lamb tells him to be cautious of the crab apples. He is embarrassed and tries to run away from there because he feels that like the others Mr Lamb would poke fun at his scarred face.

Derry is surprised to note that Mr Lamb welcomes him to his garden and believes him when he says that he had not come to steal the apples. Mr Lamb instils confidence in him when he tells Derry that he not so frightening. Derry is impressed by the old man's talk about beauty and beast, pretty girls and the plain talk of about how the world will change its attitude towards Derry. Mr Lamb's concept of the world, friendship, not believing everything one hears, the story about the timid man who locked himself and the like sound peculiar to Derry but interest him. He understands the underlying message that Mr Lamb is giving him.

He is encouraged by Mr Lamb's words, "You'll get on the way you want, like all the rest." Gradually, Derry is able to shed his inhibitions, insecurities, fears and complexes. The talk with Mr Lamb is the beginning of his transformation. That's the reason why Derry says, "....you don't know what I could do." Mr Lamb makes him understand the true meaning of life.

Thus, Derry is drawn towards Mr Lamb because both of them have suffered loss and humiliation and both feel isolated and lonely.

Question 2. In which section of the play does Mr Lamb display signs of loneliness and disappointment? What are the ways in which Mr Lamb tries to overcome these feelings?

Answer Mr Lamb lives all alone in a huge house with a large garden. He has no one for company, neither his family nor friends. Inspite of this, he is happy because the neighbourhood children come to his garden for scrumping apples and pears. They tease him by calling him 'Lamey-Lamb' but he does not mind their mockery.

Anybody who enters the open gates of his house is heartily welcomed by Mr Lamb. That's the reason why he keeps his doors and windows open for anyone to come in. He loves to give the jelly and toffee he makes to children and watch them playing in his garden. He says, "There's nothing God has made that doesn't interest me". Everything that belongs to him also belongs to the others.

There is ample evidence in the story to prove that he feels lonely and isolated. He longs for somebody to talk to. At the end of scene one, we hear Mr Lamb telling himself, "We all know. I'll come back. They never do, though. Not them. Never do they come back". This is the time when Derek wants to rush home as he thinks his mother will be worried. That's when Mr Lamb says the above lines. Although Derek promises to come back Mr Lamb does not believe him. He simply walks away to look after his bees.

The words spoken by Mr Lamb reveal his deepest feelings of loneliness. Although Derek does come back but it is too late for Mr Lamb does not and cannot long for any company now.

Question 3. The actual pain or inconvenience caused by a physical impairment is often much less than the sense of alienation felt by the person with disabilities. What is the kind of behaviour that the person expects from others?

Answer Mr Lamb and Derek both are victims of physical impairment. Mr Lamb has an artificial leg made of tin and Derek has scarred face. Undoubtedly, both have suffered humiliations in life on account of their handicaps.

Derek, however, suffers not only from his handicap but also from low self-esteem, lack of confidence, desolation and withdrawal. He feels that nobody wants him or loves him. His family is also not concerned about him. Even his mother loves and kisses him only because she has to. Moreover, she does not kiss him on the side of the face which has scars.

Derek does not like meeting people because he hates their sermonizing attitude. He knows that their sympathetic talk is insincere. It does not arise out of compassion but pity. They fear looking at his ugly face.

Looking at Derek's example, we feel that people with physical impairment need genuine concern. They can perform better than average individuals who do not suffer from any disability provided they get the right opportunities to prove themselves.

The need of the hour is not to marginalise them but intensify efforts to bring them into the mainstream. They are an indispensable part of the society who need appreciation and encouragement to stand on their own feet.

Question 4. Will Derry get back to his old seclusion or will Mr Lamb's brief association effect a change in the kind of life he will lead in the future?

Answer When Derry meets Mr Lamb he is a fourteen years old boy who has lost all zest for life. He has lost all self-regard and suffers from a terrible inferiority complex due to his scarred face. He hates meeting people and remains withdrawn.

After meeting Mr Lamb, Derry is filled with enthusiasm for life. Mr Lamb's words have a profound effect on him and he changes drastically. He is not overtly conscious of his ugly face. We get a reflection of Derry's transformation in Scene Two when he reaches his house after a brief encounter with Mr Lamb. Mr Lamb, his friend, philosopher and guide has had a great impact on his psyche. He tells his mother, "you shouldn't believe all you hear". He categorically tells her that he wants to go back to Mr Lamb to listen to bees singing and him talking. He says that Mr Lamb talks to him about, "Things that matter. Things nobody else has ever said. Things I want to think about."

In the end, he rushes to meet his mentor to keep his promise to the old man. Looking at these developments one is bound to conclude that Derry will not become secluded once again. His brief association with Mr Lamb has left an indelible imprint on him and he will base his later life on the teachings of Mr Lamb. He'll know whom to believe and what to hear. I am sure that Derek will lead a confident and happy existence in the future.

How about... (Page 69)

Using your imagination to suggest another ending to the above story?

Answer The above story can be changed slightly to end on a happy note. It can happen that Derry will make efforts to revive Mr Lamb instead of weeping. Mr Lamb regains consciousness, gets up with Derry's assistance and invites Derry to meet him regularly so that Derry can learn more about living a better life from him. Derry is overjoyed and promises to do so.

7

Evans Tries an O-Level

Colin Dexter

Introduction

"Evens Tries An O-Level" is an absorbing story about ingenuity of a prisoner, James Roderick Evans from a jail in Oxford. The story holds the reader in its grip firmly as inspite of the all out efforts of the prison officials, Evans makes a dexterous escape right under their nose.

He makes a masterplan and executes it so efficiently that he is escorted out of the prison by the officials themselves! At one point in the story, he is caught by the Governor himself but he manages to elude him skilfully. The story is a vivid narration of the battle of wits between the authorities and the criminal.

The Story

The Governor makes request for conduct of exam

The Governor of Oxford Prison calls on the Secretary of the Examination Board on telephone in early March. The call is regarding one of his prisoners, James Evans, who wants to appear in O-level German Examination to be held on June 8. After having discussions on the examinee's nature, the examination room, the security there, the candidate remaining 'incommunicado', the secretary agrees to send one of the parsons from St Mary Mags to act as an invigilator.

Evans teacher wishes him good luck

Evans started night classes in O-level German last September and according to the Governor, "He's dead keen to get some sort of academic qualification".

Evans is called 'Evans the Break' by the prison officers because thrice he had escaped from the prison. Although he is 'just a congenital kleptomaniac', he is a quiet but sharp man. His German tutor wishes him good luck for the examination on June 7 but tells him clearly that he has hardly any chance of getting through. Surprisingly, Evans says, "I may surprise everybody". This prepares the reader for some exciting events to follow.

The examination day; prison officials take precaution

At 8.30 am on the examination day, two prison offices, Jackson and a new recruit, Stephens visit Evans. Jackson is aware of the inventive and unconventional skills of Evans and calls him 'our little Einstein' They both know each others tactics well and so does the author, Colin Dexter calls them 'warm enemies'. Jackson tells Stephens to take away the razor after Evans is done with his shaving.

Jackson particularly points out Evans's dirty red and white 'bobble hat' but does not insist on taking it off as Evans considers it his lucky charm. Evans is visibly annoyed because his scissors and nail-filer have been taken away. At this Jackson tells him that he has acted on the instructions given by the Governor. Evans is told curtly that there's just half an hour left for the examination to start and he is advised to hurry up.

Reverend Stuart McLeery; conditions in Evans' cell

At about the same time when Evans was busy getting ready for the examination, Reverend Stuart McLeery stepped out of his flat. He was carrying all the necessary things for the smooth conduct of the exam, a sealed question paper envelope, a yellow invigilation form, a special 'authentication' card from the Examinations Board, a paper knife, a Bible and 'The Church Times'.

In the prison cell as Evans is busy shaving himself, Stephens makes some preparations for the conduct of the examination. He brings in two chairs and places them before the table near the cell door. Jackson warns Evans to behave himself.

Evans asks him why has he been put in that particular cell that has been bugged did the prison authorities really think that he is going to do something wrong. Jackson approves of the Governor's action because he says that nobody will take any chance with a prisoner like Evans. He further clarifies that the Governor himself will be listening to each and every conversation going on in the cell.

The examination begins at 9.25 am

Reverend McLeery, who is the invigilator, makes his entry into the prison and is taken to Evans' cell who is concentrating hard on a book of elementary German Grammar.

At 9.10 am, the Governor switches on the receiver. He knows in his heart of hearts that all these precautions were redundant because if Evans had to make an escape, he could have easily done so from the Recreation Block. Still he feels that it is not wise to take any chances. He believes that "Evans was as safe as houses..." Suddenly he decides to tell his officers to search McLeery.

McLeery's suitcase is 'riffled cursorily though'. The presence of a small semi-inflated rubber ring surprises the officers but they are courteously informed that McLeery is suffering from piles and the rubber ring helps him in sitting in a particular position for a long time. The officers feel satisfied and the invigilator is allowed to go into cell.

McLeery gives necessary instructions to the candidate regarding writing down the paper's name 021-1, index number 313 and the centre number 271. Stephens is in the cell until now but Evans does not like his presence. The Governor asks Jackson to call him out. Finally, the examination begins at 9.25 am.

A correction in the question paper

At 9.40 am, the Assistant Secretary for modern languages informs the Governor about the correction slip not being put in the examination package. The Governor takes all necessary precautions and Evans is told about the corrections on page three, line fifteen by the invigilator.

At 10.50 am there is a request from Evans that he be allowed to put a blanket around his shoulders as he was feeling cold. He is granted the request Stephens notices this development but later on does not bother too much because he feels that some of the cells are quite cold.

A call from the Governor for Stephens

Three minutes before the examination was to get over, Jackson calls Stephens telling him that the Governor wants to speak to him. The Governor instructs Stephens to accompany McLeery personally to the main gate. As both the them head towards the main gate, Stephens has an illusion that the invigilator had suddenly grown thinner. The Scottish accent seemed more noticeable than before.

He suddenly thinks that he must have one last look at Evans. He is in for a surprise. Stephens sees a man sprawled back in Evans' chair with the blanket slipping from his shoulders. His closely cropped hair was splattered with blood. Stephens and Jackson thought that it was McLeery who had been hit by Evans. Evans has, thus, escaped. (Actually it is not so).

The wounded man spills out Evans' secret

The wounded man in Evans' cell whom everybody thought to be McLeery tells the prison authorities not to worry about him. He desperately and restlessly tells the Governor about the photocopied sheet that had been 'superimposed over the last (originally blank) page of the question paper,' where a few words were written in German. It instructed Evans to adhere to the plan strictly and not to hit McLeery too hard. It said that the three minutes before the examination are very important. He is also instructed not to over do the Scottish accent.

Detective Superintendent Carter swings into action. McLeery is, however, very agitated and tells them that Evans has gone towards Elsfield Way. The Governor asks Carter to take McLerry with him because he is the only one who knows what has happened really.

The Governor takes officers to task

The Governor now scolds his officers for behaving foolishly and calls them 'two morons' because he had not made any call at 11.22 am *i.e.,* three minutes before the examination time was to get over. At that time the Governor was trying to get in touch with the Examinations Board.

Jackson is taken to task because of his negligence. He had not searched the cell thoroughly the previous evening. This resulted in Evans concealing the 'clerical paraphernalia'. Thereafter, the Governor looks at the photocopied slip and thinks of Newbury. He orders the driver to take Jackson and Stephens to St Aldates Police Station to meet Chief Inspector, Bell. The Governor thinks about Evans and appreciates his ingenuity. He considers leaving the question paper behind a mistake because it is this that is going to lead him to 'Mr clever-clever Evans.'

Meanwhile Carter informs him that McLeery had seen Evans driving off along Elsfield way. He was given a chase but they somehow missed him. The Governor tells him that he believes that Evans is heading towards Newbury and gives reasons for his belief.

The real truth; McLeery is held hostage in his flat

When the Governor asks Carter about McLeery, Carter tells him that the parson was left at Radcliffe hospital. When the Governor rings up the hospital he finds out that McLeery had escaped.

At this point in the story, the Governor is sure that something is indeed terribly wrong. He rushes to the flat of the parson only to find him bound and gagged in his study. He has been there since 8.15 am, Eventually, everybody comes to know that Evans impersonating McLeery had stayed in the prison itself.

Evans as a free man

The author once again makes us meet Evans who is a free man now through a dexterous turn of events. Evans has escaped from the prison the fourth time now. He regrets cutting his long hair but considers himself fortunate that he was not asked to take off his hat in the cell. He decides to go back to his hotel room. On his way to the room, he appreciates McLeery's plan of wearing double minister's dress. As he enters the room, he is shocked to find the Governor in his hotel room.

The Governor tries to defeat Evans at his own game

A 'visibly shaken' Evans tells the Governor that it is the correction slip that did him in. The Governor tells him how he reached the hotel room. The index number 313 and centre number 271 referred to the area where Evans could be.

Evans, similarly, tells him about the skill in getting the blood to splatter on the head. Actually, the rubber ring contained pig's blood!

The Governor enquires how could Evans plan out everything when he had no visitors. A delighted Evans tells him "I've got lots of friends, though". The German teacher was one of them and he was of immense help to him.

Finally, Evans is brought out of his hotel room. He is handcuffed by the prison officer and the two of them "clamber awkwardly into the back seat of the prison van". The Governor tells Evans, "See you soon" but it appears that Evans has some other plans in store.

Evans makes the final escape

The moment the Governor is out of sight, the prison officer (actually a friend of Evans) unlocks the handcuffs and asks the driver to drive fast Evans tells him to turn to Newbury.

Thus, the Governor and his officers are completely outwitted by the clever Evans who manages to engineer an escape even after being caught!

Exercises

Before you read   (Page 70)

Should criminals in prison be given the opportunity of learning and education?

Answer Yes, they should. No one should be denied the opportunity of learning and education. If prison inmates are provided with education and work skills, they will become responsible citizens by turning towards a better future without the need for committing crimes.

Read and find out   (Page 70)

Question 1. What kind of a person was Evans?

Answer Evans was exceptionally cunning, crafty and elusive. He escaped under the nose of officials and security. He was known as "Evans the Break" among the prison officers because he had escaped from the prison thrice. He looked scruffy and unshaven with a heavy Scottish accent. He appeared in the O-level German examination as a part of a well planned strategy to fool the prison staff.

Question 2. What were the precautions taken for the smooth conduct of the examination?

Answer Tight security arrangements and probable arrangements were made for the smooth conduct of the examination. Senior prison officer Jackson, Officer Stephen and the Governor himself worked round the clock. A person from St Mary Mags was to invigilate. The Secretary accepted the unusual request of the Governor to conduct the examination in the Evan's cell.

(Page 77)

Question 3. Will the exam now go as scheduled?

Answer The two hour examination was to start at 9:15 am, but it got a little late in the underway. All the more the examination was interrupted at 9:40 am to inform about a correction slip which was not placed beforehand.

(Page 81)

Question 4. Did the Governor and his staff finally heave a sigh of relief?

Answer The Governor and his staff initially had a sigh of relief when they announced, 'Stop writing please' at 11:25 am as the examination was now over. But their relief did not stay for long when they found that Evans had made a fool out of them again and escaped in a disguised manner under their nose.

(Page 84)

Question 5. Will the injured McLeery be able to help the prison officers track Evans?

Answer The injured McLeery in no way helped the prison officers to track Evans because he was Evans himself disguised as McLeery. He rather confused the staffs by directing them to Elsfield way to track Evans so that he could escape from there web.

(Page 85)

Question 6. Will the clues left behind on the question paper, put Evans back in prison again?

Answer The clue of the six figure reference 313/271 on the question paper was enough to trace Evans. He was traced in the hotel room and was being taken to the prison but finally he escaped in the prison van.

(Page 86)

Question 7. Where did Evans go?

Answer After escaping from the prison, Evans enjoyed a stroll at Chipping Norton. From there, he decided to return to the Golden Lion. He collected the keys from the hotel reception and walked up to his room where he was shocked and frozen to find the Governor sitting on the narrow bed.

Reading with insight   (Page 92)

Question 1. Reflecting on the story, what do you feel about Evans' having the last laugh?

Answer From the beginning of the story, we feel that the prison authorities are not taking any chances with Evans. Evans, on the other hand, is leaving no stone unturned to make a fool out of them.

The authorities do not bother to check the antecedents of the German teacher at first. Secondly, although they bug the cell, take away anything which could be a potential weapon for Evans including his nail-scissors, nail file and shaving accessories, he manages to outsmart them. The reason he gives for putting on his hat will not point a finger against him. He manages to get Stephens out of the cell and avoid his prying eyes at regular intervals.

He manages to evade the officers and gives them a slip by impersonating McLeery. The trick he uses to splatter blood on his head is interesting. It takes a while for the officers to realise that Evans is actually in the cell and has escaped from the hospital. Evans frustrates and flusters the officers who finally catch him at the hotel but this is a part of a greater conspiracy. Gullible as the Governor is, he thinks that he has nabbed "Mr clever-clever Evans" but Evans manages to escape right under his nose. Then, the officer in the prison van is also an accomplice of Evans and he is successful in dodging the Governor yet again.

Thus, the officers are reduced to a bunch of 'good-for-a-giggle' officers who are outwitted by the scheming Evans and his clever friends at very step.

Question 2. When Stephens comes back to the cell he jumps to a conclusion and the whole machinery blindly goes by his assumption without even checking the identity of the injured 'McLeery'. Does this show how hasty conjectures can prevent one from seeing the obvious? How is the criminal able to predict such negligence?

Answer Evans has the insight to judge others characters and this is what he does with officers in the prison. He knows that Jackson has a soft corner and thus, he takes his advantage by concealing his cropped hair with the hat. The Governor is also befooled by Evans. For once even the Governor starts thinking that he is "dead keen to get some sort of a qualification." Going by the events in then story we can say that Evans is a plotter who knows the moves of authorities too well.

The story, undoubtedly proves that hasty conjectures can prevent one from seeing the obvious. This is because they affect our ability to think clearly and logically. This is the reason why, perhaps, nobody questions that how there could be two parsons; one in the cell and the other who has been escorted by Stephens out of the prison premises.

The entire machinery including the Governor, is shocked to see 'McLeery' in a pool of blood. In this utter confusion, all hell breaks loose. The Governor tells Carter, the detective Superintendent to take 'McLeery' (actually it is Evans) along with him because he is the only one who knows what is going on. Evans escapes from the hospital. The question paper is left behind deliberately to mislead the Governor and him.

When the Governor comes face to face with Evans, he escapes right under his nose. Evans is a perfect plotter and a manipulator who expected such a reaction from the these 'good-for-a-giggle' officers. He had monitored their behaviour for a long time and knew that they would panic under the circumstances. Thus, Evans rightly predicted their moves.

Question 3. What could the Governor have done to securely bring back Evans to prison when he caught him at the Golden Lion? Does the final act of foolishness really prove that "he was just another good-for-a-giggle, gullibe governor, that was all"?

Answer   Since the beginning, the Governor was apprehensive about Evans. Evans had been a habitual jail breaker and the Governor knew from the start how sharp Evans was; courtesy his past escapades. Although he had taken all precautions for the successful conduct of the examination, Evans played his game successfully since the very beginning. The Governor felt that Evans should be given a chance to study. Evans took advantage of the emotional side of the Governor by planting his accomplice in disguise of the German teacher.

Evans built up the whole strategy step by step and outwitted the prison authorities including the Governor. He had such a psychological insight into his opponents that even when he was finally caught at the Golden Lion, he was confident that he will handle the situation deftly.

On the Governor's part, he committed a grave blunder when after rearresting Evans he handed him over to the 'silent prison officer'. He should have verified his credentials or handed such a sharp criminal like Evans to a capable and known officer. The Governor should have checked the people in the van because it is obvious from the developments in the story that they were not reliable people. For instance, as soon as the Governor is out of sight, the prison officer unlocks Evans's handcuffs and the driver asks for instructions regarding the direction to go. Thus, we can say that the Governor himself is responsible for the final escape of Evans and proves rightly that, "he was just another good-for-a-giggle, gullible Governor, that was all".

Question 4. While we condemn the crime, we are sympathetic to the criminal. Is this the reason why prison staff often develop a soft corner for those in custody?

Answer   Yes, it is a fact that although we hate crime but we have a soft corner for the criminal. This is the case with Evans also. Although the Governor is conversant with his past record and escapades, he does not want to deprive Evans of an opportunity to learn. Similarly, the author describes the relationship between Evans and Jackson as that of 'warm enemies'. Jackson is kind-hearted and that's the reason why he allows Evans to wear his hat during the exam as the latter said that it was his good luck charm.

Evans's tender heart and his affectionate side is seen and appreciated by the staff. He is an active participant in Christmas plays, is good at imitating people but not known to be violent. Even the Governor does not like to believe that Evans is planning to escape once again.

From Evans's example, it is seen that even the prison authorities do not like to treat the prisoners harshly. With time even they develop a liking and a rapport with them.

Question 5. Do you agree that between crime and punishment it is mainly a battle of wits?

Answer   Yes, there is a fierce battle of wits between crime and punishment. The one who outdo's the another wins the battle hands down.

Evans and the prison authorities are incessantly involved in a battle of wits. It's a neck to neck race where finally, Evans and his accomplices steal the show. Meticulous planners, they foresee and predict things. They are even able to know beforehand how their opponents will react in a particular situation.

For example, Evans knows that Jackson has a soft corner for him and takes full advantage of the situation by getting permission to keep his hat on. The Governor and Evans particularly leave no stone unturned in proving each other their superior. The Governor takes utmost precautions to render Evan's manoeuvres ineffective like bugging the cell during the examination, figuring the hotel out but in this particular instance it is Evans and his friends who call the shots. The authorities are, indeed reduced to a bunch of 'good-for-a-giggle' officers.

8

Memories of Childhood

Zitkala-Sa and Bama

Introduction

This unit presents two autobiographical episodes from the lives of two women from marginalised communities. The anecdotes belong to their childhood and have left a lasting impact on their psyche.

Zitkala-Sa in her works criticised dogma and dedicated her lift to the evils of oppression. This Native American woman is highly critical of the Carlisle Indian School and this episode from the unit highlights the same.

Bama, on the other hand, is a Tamil Dalit woman from a Roman Catholic family. Her anecdote here challenges the age-old practice of untouchability and the caste system.

The Story Retold

I. The Cutting of My Long Hair

Zitkala-Sa ....

The narrator recounts the first day in Carlisle School

The first day in the school was a bitter and cold day with snow all around. She finds the breakfast bell jarring and disagreeable. The clatter of shoes on the bare floors annoyed her. The cocophony of noises disturb her and she longs for freedom.

The immodestly dressed girls

The narrator understands that a pale faced white-haired woman supervised and inspected the girls. The girls march into the dining room along with the Indian girls. They wore 'closely clinging dresses' and stiff shoes. The small girls wore shingled hair and sleeved aprons. The narrator feels uncomfortable in her dress as it kept slipping. She is surprised to find that the girls did not seem to mind their dresses or hair. She also sees three native boys who marched in from the opposite door. The narrator really felt uneasy there.

The breakfast time

The narrator heard a bell and every student pulled a chair from under the table. The narrator, however, pulls a chair and sits down. She notices that all other students sit down at the ringing of the second bell. She hears a man muttering the prayer. While the narrator was having a good view of the surroundings, the other students sat with their heads hung down. The pale-faced woman was looking sternly at her. The narrator's eyes are downcast and she hears the ringing of the third bell. She understands that the third bell is meant to start eating. The narrator is pained by her strange surroundings and this weird 'eating by formula'. She feels helpless and cries.

The narrator's friend Judewin; the narrator puts up a fight

The narrator's friend Judewin knew a few words of English and she had overheard the pale faced woman saying that her long and heavy hair would be cut. The narrator is suddenly reminded of her mother's words who said that only the hair of prisoners of war were shingled by capturers. Short hair were worn by mourners and shingled hair by cowards. Judewin decided to give in her opponents because 'they were strong'. On the other hand, the narrator says, "No, I will not submit! I will struggle first!"

To escape her fate, the narrator creeps upstairs unnoticed. She enters a large room and crawls under the bed in the dark room. She hears loud calls for her in the hall and sounds of approaching feet. Women and girls enter the room and search for her everywhere. Somebody throws up the window curtains and there is light in the room. A girl notices her under the bed. Despite her fierce resistance, the narrator is dragged out, carried downstairs and tied to a chair.

Gnawing off the narrator's hair

The narrator's resistance was of little help. She could feel the cold blades of sciessors against her neck and this made her lose her spirit. She felt anguished and pained. "Since the day I was taken from my mother I had suffered extreme indignities." The narrator thinks that she has been like a wooden puppet who is being tossed about in the air. She is really distressed by the fact that nobody came to comfort her. She misses her mother very much and feels like an animal driven by a herder.

II. We Too Are Human Being

Bama ....

Untouchability and the narrator

The narrator takes us back to the days when she was a class-third student. At that time, she had not heard people speak of untouchability but had felt humiliated by what it is.

The narrator walks back home from school

Reminiscencing about her escapades from school, the narrator says that she used to take half an hour to one hour to walk back home from school. Actually, she should have covered the distance in ten minutes. She watched all the fun, games, novelties and shops on the way. She enjoyed the monkey antics, saw a snake displayed by a snake charmer and a cycle pedalist who kept pedalling for three days continuously. she also crossed the Maariyaata temple on the way and saw Pongal offering being cooked.

The narrator witnessed a variety of other interesting things on the way. She heard politicians with their persuasive speeches and saw street plays, puppet shows and stunt performances. The narrator liked to see the coffee clubs on the way, the waiter's act of cooling coffee, the onions being chopped. She also observed the almond trees and their fallen fruit. The market was full of seasonal fruits, vegetables and other scrumptious delicacies. All these activities interested her and delayed her coming back home.

The landlord and his activities

One day the narrator saw the landlord sitting on a raised platform. She saw him supervising the proceedings of the people of her caste, who were driving the cattle round and round to tread out grain from the straw. She also saw that the animals had been muzzled so that they do not eat the straw. This seemed to be a funny sight and the narrator thoroughly enjoyed watching it.

The elder with a small packet

Meanwhile the narrator noticed an elder of their street. He carried a small packet of *vadais* or green banana bhajji, holding it with a string. He walked in such a strange manner that the narrator felt like laughing. He carried the packet by its string, without touching it. The elder crouched while hading over the packet to the landlord. Mannerless as the landlord is, he ate the *vadais* without offering it to anyone.

The narrator's conversation with the elder brother

The narrator told the elder brother about their elder's comic behaviour. Annan told her that the landlord belonged to an upper caste and considered them of a low caste. He wouldn't touch lower caste people. The narrator felt really sad on hearing it. She wondered how the *vadai* would get polluted when it was first wrapped in a banana leaf and then parcelled in paper. She felt provoked and angry. She says, "The thought of it infuriated me". She really detested the idea of the people of her caste doing petty errands for the upper caste people.

Annan's advice to the narrator

The elder brother of the narrator was a university student and he visited home during the holidays. He advised her to study hard because "...... if we study and make progress, we can throw away these indignities." He advised her to, "Work hard and learn". Annan's words left a lasting impression on the girl's mind and she stood first in the class. Consequently many people became her friends.

Exercises

Reading with insight (Page 100)

Question 1. The two accounts that you read above are based in two distant cultures. What is the commonality of theme found in both of them?

Answer Oppression and exploitation of the indigenous people, women and the weak is the harsh reality of all countries and civilizations throughout the world. In a similar vein, the struggle of these marginalised people is something we all can identify with.

There is a thread of commonality running between the accounts of both Zitkala-Sa and Bama. The only difference between them is the time gap and their vastly different cultures. Zitkala-Sa is a native American who belongs to the late 19th century, where as Bama is a prominent Dalit writer belonging to the contemporary era. Zitkala-Sa belonged to a marginalised community which was exploited to the hilt. Her identity was questioned throughout and finally taken away from her. Bama on the other hand, is a victim of untouchability, casteism and vehement discrimination.

Zitkala-Sa was forcibly taken to a school where an alien language and culture was thrusted upon her. Her long hair was chopped off against her wishes and the regimental life that she had to accustom herself to contained her free spirit. Her moccasins were also forcibly taken away from her and she was given stiff shoes to wear.

Similarly, Bama realised very early in life that she belonged to the community of untouchables. Her elders have to crouch before the upper caste people and carry out petty errands for them silently.

Another common thread running through both the stories is the response of the protagonists. Both believe in putting up a stiff fight. Zitkala-Sa resists against chopping off her hair but ultimately is overpowered by the school authorities. Thus, she is helpless but later on, through her writings continues fighting against oppression.

Bama is infuriated at the sight of her elder carrying a packet of *vadais* by its string for the landlord just because mere touch would pollute them. She feels like touching the *vadais* herself! She wonders why do the people of her community have to serve the upper caste unquestioningly. She is helpless because she can't stop this unjustified practice. Even she carried on her fight through her revolutionary writings.

Question 2. It may take a long time for oppression to be resisted, but the seeds of rebellion are sowed very early in life. Do you agree that injustice in any form cannot escape being noticed even by children?

Answer   The history of any country is replete with instances of oppression by the people in power and the landed classes. It takes a while for individuals to understand the situation but when they do, it results in a revolution. Zitkala-Sa and Bama, both were school going children when they witnessed rough treatment being meted out to themselves or their community.

Zitkala-Sa, a Native American is humiliated and stripped of her long hair by the colonial masters. Her moccasins are also forcibly taken away and she is subjected to a regimental life that stifles her. Bama, is a Tamil Dalit. An elder of her community is subjected to insults by a landlord and he carries out his orders meekly just because he belongs to a low caste.   Both these episodes in "Memories of Childhood" highlight class distinction, suppression and class struggle.

Both episodes prove that injustice in any form does not escape notice even by children. Zitkala-Sa revolts and resists against the school authorities with all her might because she does not want her hair to be shingled like that of a coward's. Bama puts up a fight by bringing laurels to her community through her school achievements. Thus, she proves that she is superior to the so called upper caste. So, it is rightly proved that children know of injustice and react to them in their own unique ways.

Question 3. Bama's experience is that of a victim of the caste system. What kind of discrimination does Zitkala-Sa's experience depict? What are their responses to their respective situations?

Answer Bama is a Tamil Dalit who is a victim of class distinction and exploitation. On the other hand, Zitkala-Sa was an American Indian, that is, she belonged to the community of Native Americans who were unduly victimized and plundered by their colonial masters. They were stripped of their culture and their identity was altered with.

Zitkala-Sa was forcibly put in a place which was very cold for her. She did not like the loud, jarring noise of the bell and the incessant murmuring in an alien language. 'Eating by formula' detests her completely. In her community, long hair is very much valued. Short hair is worn by mourners and cowards. So when her hair is shingled, she feels devastated because according to her mother only cowards have shingled, hair. She tries hard to resist but ultimately is overpowered by the authorities. She has to fit in into 'closely clinging' dresses and stiff shoes. Lonely in an alien culture she misses her mother and says with extreme regret, "Since the day I was taken from my mother I had suffered extreme indignities". She feels helpless and that's the reason why she has been tossed about in the air like a wooden puppet. She rightly says, "I was only one of many little animals driven by a herder".

Zitkala-Sa's suffering is a saga of her community's struggle against all odds. Their native culture, value systems are under threat from an alien culture which they need to safegaurd.

Both the writers, Zitkala-Sa and Bama resist the efforts of their exploiters to victimize and oppress them. Zitkala-Sa continues her marathon efforts to fight against an unknown cultural set-up through her writings. Bama brought in a freshness and newness in her writings in her efforts a timed at trying to change the attitude of the upper castes. She outclassed her foes through her hard work and zeal.